QUICK-BUT-GREAT
Science Fair Projects

Shar Levine and
Leslie Johnstone

illustrated by Emily S. Edliq

Sterling Publishing Co., Inc.
New York

To Elsa, Harry, Sara, Yidgal, El'ad, and Tamir. Thanks for your love and encouragement. — S. L.

To the Sharfs, Holly, Roger, Emily, and Kyle. Thanks for your love, support, and kind words. — L. J.

To my dear Granny and Granddad for helping me realize a long-held dream — and for the many years of delightful correspondence. And to the Coons family for your constant kindness and friendship. — E. E.

To my mother with love. — J. C.

Acknowledgments

The authors are grateful for the support and assistance of Science World, Vancouver, B.C. Without the help of Jim Wiese and Matt Stewart, the really cool bed of nails picture would not have been possible. Lest we forget, thanks to Charles Ng in the gift shop.

Thanks also to Susan Lawson of the City of Vancouver, Board of Parks and Public Recreation, Sunset Nursery, for her loan of the *Mimosa pudica* and the weird seed pods, and to Dr. Peter Cooperberg, of the University of British Columbia. Thanks again to Dr. David Hawes and his son Peter for the loan of the completed science fair display. Great work!

As always, Dr. Elaine Humphrey, head of the E.M. Lab at the University of British Columbia, came to our rescue and allowed us to photograph the lab and provided the photomicrographs and dandelion seed and Sundew photos. Elaine, you are the best! And to Andrew and Tobias: you may not want to admit it, but you inspired this book. Finally, to Jeff Connery and Emily Edliq: you make us look good.

Library of Congress Cataloging-in-Publication Data

Levine, Shar, 1953-
    Quick-but-great science fair projects / Shar Levine and Leslie Johnstone ; illustrated by Emily S. Edliq.
      p. cm.
    Includes index.
    Summary: Provides information on the basics of science fair projects and suggestions for a variety of projects using easily obtainable materials.
    ISBN 0-8069-5939-8
    1. Science projects—Juvenile literature. [1. Science projects. 2. Science—Experiments. 3. Experiments.]
I. Johnstone, Leslie. II. Edliq, Emily S., ill. III. Title.

Q182.3 .L38 2000
507'.8—dc21

99-087162

1 3 5 7 9 10 8 6 4 2

Published by Sterling Publishing Company, Inc.
387 Park Avenue South, New York, N.Y. 10016
©2000 by Shar Levine and Leslie Johnstone
Distributed in Canada by Sterling Publishing
℅ Canadian Manda Group, One Atlantic Avenue, Suite 105
Toronto, Ontario, Canada M6K 3E7
Distributed in Great Britain and Europe by Cassell PLC
Wellington House, 125 Strand, London WC2R 0BB, England
Distributed in Australia by Capricorn Link (Australia) Pty Ltd.
P.O. Box 6651, Baulkham Hills, Business Centre, NSW 2153, Australia
Printed in China
All rights reserved

Sterling ISBN 0-8069-5939-8

Contents

PREFACE 4

How to Use This Book 4

Hints for Teachers 5

Science Celebrations 7

Hints for Parents 8

Note to Kids 9

LET'S GET STARTED 10

How to Find a Topic 11

Should I Work with My Best Friend? 12

How to Find an Expert 12

Types of Projects 14

The Scientific Method 15

PRESENTING YOUR PROJECT 20

Tables, Graphs, and Charts 20

How to Write a Report 22

The Display 24

The Oral Presentation 28

What Do the Judges Look For? 30

PROJECTS 32

Safety First 32

Nothing to Sneeze At 34

Genetic Printing 36

Got Milk? 39

Scents of Smell 41

The Yolk's on You 43

The Sensitive Plant 46

Which Way Did It Go? 49

Leafy Greens 51

Seeds of Change 53

Pine Cone Hygrometers 56

Some Like It Hot 58

The Iceman Cometh 60

Bubbleology 62

Shake, Rattle, and Roll 64

Bull's-Eye 66

Tracing the Stars 71

Oil Slick 73

Down the Drain 75

Something Old, Something New 77

What Counts? 80

Bed of Nails 83

Will It Fly? 86

Weigh to Go 89

Magnetic Erasers 91

Streamlined 93

INDEX 96

PREFACE

This book was inspired by our friend Andrew and his son Tobias. One day, Andrew telephoned in a panic. His son had a science fair project due on Monday, and the experiment he had chosen wouldn't work. "Could you and your writing partner help?" he pleaded. "Make it do something!" Recognizing the anguish in his voice, we pitched in and soon had the activity organized.

Andrew is not alone. Throughout the world, wherever there are science fairs, frustrated parents and anxious children can find themselves in a similar predicament. Sometimes kids leave science fair projects for the weekend before they are due. Sometimes they plan an experiment, only to discover that they can't get it to work. Sometimes students choose a topic that is too difficult or too overwhelming and they have to find something simpler at the last minute.

This book is designed to help teachers, parents, and students not only make it through science fairs, but also enjoy the experience.

HOW TO USE THIS BOOK

Most of the experiments in this book can be done in a day. Even the longest projects in the book only take about two weeks. The research will take you a few days more. The actual writing won't take you too long.

This book is divided into two parts. Read the first part of this book, pages 4 to 33. This will give you the background you need before you start your research. Once you have done that, skim the experiments in the second part. These are meant to give you some direction, and ideas for projects.

Each experiment is designed to give you enough information to perform the science fair project described, or you can develop one based on the ideas raised in the book.

We have not told you what is going to happen in the experiments, as the most important aspect of science fair projects is to perform the experiments and make the observations yourself!

The opening paragraphs of each experiment are an introduction to the experiment, which tell you a little about the experiment, to perhaps make you interested in examining this project.

The TITLE is an example of what you might wish to call your experiment for the science fair project.

The PURPOSE is the general problem you are going to investigate.

The HYPOTHESIS is an assumption you make, which you test by doing the project. Your hypothesis may be different from the one given in the book.

The MATERIALS section includes the basic materials you can use to perform the experiment. Yours may be quite different from ours, if

you decide to look at a different aspect of the problem.

The RESEARCH SOURCES AND RELATED TOPICS section in each project gives you suggestions about where to look for more information, and some of the key words or ideas to research. You will have to do your own research for each of the projects.

In the PROCEDURE section, you will get step-by-step instructions for one project. You may choose to investigate some of the other questions discussed in the project and think of your own way to do other experiments.

As for the RESULTS, they depend on YOU! This section contains questions to guide your discussion of the results. Depending on your results, you may have questions of your own that need answering.

If you need some DISPLAY HINTS, check out this section of the project. See page 28 for things you can and can't display.

Instead of doing the project in the book, you may want to go ahead and try one of the extra project suggestions in GOING FURTHER at the end of each project. If you are in grades 3 to 6, try one of the ideas in the ELEMENTARY LEVEL section. If you are in grades 7 to 9,

look at the ideas in the JUNIOR HIGH LEVEL section.

HINTS FOR TEACHERS

Science fairs aren't just for your students. You're a big part of their success, too. You and your students can have the best outcome if you all work together. Here are some ideas to make this a fun event.

1. Start early. If you know that a science fair is scheduled for spring, get organized in the fall. If you begin months ahead of the fair, you will have the best materials at your disposal, rather than competing with the rest of the school or even the city for books and other resources.

2. Contact other teachers for information about how to organize a science fair, and to discover the resources in your district.

3. Get help. Contact the local university or college and ask if some of the graduate students would be willing to come in for an hour or two to give advice to your class.

4. Organize a field trip to a local lab, research facility, or a company involved in scientific research.

5. Find out what the requirements are for the science fair. Contact the regional program directors for advice.

6. Set up a meeting with the national or regional science fair representatives. They will be able to walk you through the steps to a successful science fair. You can choose to be really strict and use all the criteria for the national science fair, or you can be more liberal, recognizing that some projects may not qualify for the national competition.

7. Get books like this one on how to do a science fair. Make these available for your class.

8. Spend some time on the Internet. There is an amazing amount of information on the Web. Use the words "science fair" in your search and check out the linking sites. This is a good place for topics.

9. Spend a period or two brainstorming with your class. Have them think of interesting questions to ask that would make great science fair projects.

10. No volcanos. No crystal-growing. Unless students can think of a unique way of approaching these topics, these mundane experiments should probably be avoided.

11. Have time set aside so that students can work on their science fair projects in class, where they can research, write, and ask questions.

12. Identify who will be judging the fair. If it is an experienced judge, spend time with this person, discovering what kinds of projects get the best grades.

13. Have an open discussion with your class about working alone or with a partner. Find out if your regional fair allows partnered projects. If teamed projects are allowed, examine ways of getting kids to work cooperatively. Many times, one student ends up doing all the work, while the other does not contribute significantly to the project. This can be the source of much friction and can break

up friendships. Consider prohibiting team projects.

14. Have a prejudging event in which projects are set up by each student and critiqued. This will help the student correct any deficiencies prior to the actual school science fair.

15. If you are having a science fair for the earlier grades, keep it simple. Don't expect the students to develop an experiment as if they were in the senior grades. You may wish to assign 5 topics and have each student create a science display. You may decide to hold a science celebration instead.

16. Give students a list of local suppliers of display materials. You may even get suppliers to help sponsor the event and give discounts for bulk purchases.

17. Keep copies of all the science fair project reports and the projects' outcomes — what project won, what grade each student received. If you wish, you can black out the name of the student. Over the years, you can develop your own library of science fair projects. This will be a great source of reference material.

18. Decide how you are going to grade the projects. Are you giving a grade in addition to the grade given by the judges? What percentage of the students' final mark will be given for science fair projects?

19. Create a science fair contract which will allow the

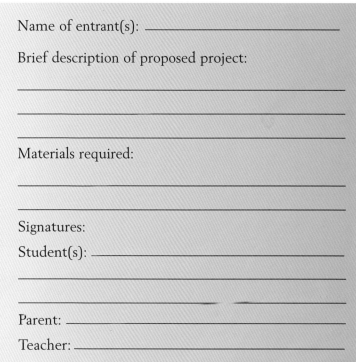

SCIENCE FAIR CONTRACT

Name of entrant(s): _____

Brief description of proposed project:

_____

_____

_____

Materials required:

_____

_____

Signatures:
Student(s): _____

_____

_____

Parent: _____

Teacher: _____

teacher, parent, and student to agree on what the project is; what parts each is responsible for; and when it needs to be completed.

SCIENCE CELEBRATIONS

Many schools feel that participating in a formal science fair is too much pressure for students in younger grades. They choose instead to host a science celebration, an event open to all interested students, in which projects are not judged. All participants receive a certificate for taking part. The projects are displayed on tables in the school gymnasium, or some other

location. Adults from the community, either parents or other volunteers, act as reviewers of the projects and allow the students to discuss their work. Autograph sheets or passports allow the students to collect the comments of reviewers. You may also wish to ask a local scientist or science teacher to perform a science demonstration for the group.

HINTS FOR PARENTS

The most difficult part of being a science fair parent can be stated in the following sentence: This is not your project! Say it like a mantra. Your child's work is going to be judged, not YOU. This is your child's project. Let your child do it. Now here's where you can help:

▶ Talk about different possibilities, but let your child choose the topic. Read the NOTE TO KIDS section to see what sources of information you can help your child to use.

▶ Set aside time to work with your child and help brainstorm ideas or build a display. There may be sharp tools or other materials that your child wants to use. It is best to closely supervise the use of any potentially dangerous items. Work with your child, but let the child make the decisions.

Fill in the target dates for each of the following:

Date of science fair: _____

Go to library or bookstore by: _____

Get 5 ideas by: _____

Decide on which project by: _____

Get project approved by: _____

Interview experts by: _____

Design project by: _____

Gather materials by: _____

Try experiment/project by: _____

First draft of project report by: _____

Final draft of report by: _____

Abstract written by: _____

Design and build display by: _____

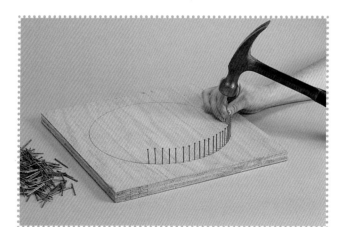

Parents can help you with tasks that are too difficult for you

▶ Help set a timetable, so that the project does not get left until the last minute.

▶ Be supportive. Do not use guilt, nag, or punish a child over a science fair project. It's supposed to be educational and fun. No matter what your child does for the science fair, tell him or her how proud you are of all the effort. It is even more important for a child to win approval from a parent than it is to win at a science fair.

Using the Internet

The Internet is one of the best places to look for information. We suggest that you place child protection programs on your Internet connection. It is also recommended that you supervise children while they are on the Net. This doesn't mean you have to hang over their shoulders, but you should be in the room with them and check from time to time on the appropriateness of the sites. Make certain no personal information is given out by your child when posting messages on any forum sites. Some of the information on the Net is based on one person's experience and may not be correct. Look to see who wrote the material posted. If there is any question about the material, check the information against another source, such as a local expert in the field.

NOTE TO KIDS

Science fairs are an inevitable part of school, just like homework and exams. Fear not, this book is here to help you. Even if you have left a science fair project until the last few days, you can still do a successful project. It's going to be fun.

Good news: You don't have to be an A student in science to get an A on a science fair project. All you need is an imagination, an inquiring mind, and some elbow grease. Here are some basic, general hints to get you going:

▶ If possible, don't leave your project to the last moment. It takes time to research, plan, and do a project. It's easier to

A kite from the "Will It Fly?" project.

get resource books when everyone else in the city is not using them, so start early.

▶ Don't get too ambitious. Try something simple but elegant. It is better to do a great job on a simpler project than a mediocre job on a complex experiment.

▶ To learn what judges look for, read the section on judges (page 30).

Doing the actual science fair project isn't that hard. It's getting started that's the most difficult part. When you haven't got a subject in mind, there is so much to choose from! Here are some guidelines to keep in mind:

1. Pick a topic that interests you. It could grow out of a hobby or something unusual you noticed. If the project is of interest, you will work harder and enjoy it more.

2. There are usually very specific guidelines about the use of living things in your research. We feel that experiments involving animals should be avoided, although many fairs allow certain types of experi-

ments with certain kinds of animals. There are rules for using people as part of your experiment also. Check with your teacher to see what the rules are for your fair before you choose a topic. Groups like the International Science and Engineering Fair (ISEF) have very specific rules and regulations about animals, human subjects, displays, and other things. Projects that do not follow the rules will not be accepted.

3. Don't be too ambitious. Choose something that you can safely accomplish in the amount of time you have. Be sure you can obtain all the equipment and supplies required when you plan your project, and that you will be able to afford them.

4. In most cases it's best to create you own science fair project. Judges reward creative thinking. Borrowing an older brother's or sister's or friend's project and just redoing it isn't a wonderful idea. If you want to build on someone else's research, you can expand a project and bring in new materials, or maybe explore another aspect of it.

5. Your project must comply with all government regulations. Be sure nothing you have planned is against the law.

A good idea for a project may be closer than you think.

HOW TO FIND A TOPIC

One of the most difficult things about doing a science fair project is finding a great topic. But the best topic may be right under your nose! We asked some students to tell us where they got their prize-winning ideas.

▶ Carol got the idea for her project from a question she had when cross-country skiing. She wondered about the effectiveness of the different ski waxes. She used an old pair of skis and strapped on weights, then

Science museums or centers are good sources of inspiration. Science World, Vancouver, Canada.

measured the time it took for the weighted skis to travel down an incline. Changing the waxes allowed her to test the effects of different types of wax.

▶ Josh spoke to a friend of his mother's who is a researcher at their local university. The professor suggested a project looking at different plant types and colors and the number of bees that were attracted to each plant.

Here are some suggestions to get you started on your topic search:

1. Visit a library or a science center. There are many books on science projects that can give you some ideas and tell you how to organize an experiment. Don't forget about zoos, planetariums, and aquariums, too!

2. If you did a science fair project last year, you may want to explore or investigate a different aspect of the topic.

3. Talk to your teacher or students at other schools. Ask them which science fair projects they liked in the past. Use that as a guideline for ideas.

4. Any scientific magazine, such as *National Geographic* or other nature magazines, electronic magazines, and sometimes consumer magazines can be great places for research and ideas.

5. Educational television, such as programs on PBS, the Discovery Channel, and other shows on science are great sources of ideas.

6. If you have access to the Internet, it is one of the best places for ideas for science fairs. There are sites for kids just like you! Many schools have Web sites, so you can access the work done by other students your age. Some libraries have Internet connections also.

7. There are sites where you can find help on the Net. You can post a message for a scientist and receive valuable assistance and guidance.

8. If you have hobbies or sports interests, you can develop a project from one of

them, as Carol did. For example, if you are interested in sculpture, you could test the effect of different amounts of water added on the texture of plaster made for castings. Or if you like to play golf, you could study the effect of dimples on the flight of golf balls.

SHOULD I WORK WITH MY BEST FRIEND?

Working with a friend can be tricky. Before you agree to any partnership, make certain that the fairs in your area permit joint projects. Having a partner can be great as long as you both share equally in the responsibilities of the project. It is not fair for one person to do all the work and for the other person to contribute little. It can cause hard feelings

and places the partner in an uncomfortable position. Don't choose a partner because he or she is an A student and you hope to raise your grade by associating yourself with this student. Choose a partner with whom you can work well, one who shares your interests.

If there is nothing prohibiting your working with a friend, or even with a team, there are several things to consider:

1. How are you going to divide up the tasks?

2. Who is responsible for making the presentation to the judges?

3. Who gets to keep the report after it is finished?

4. How are you dividing up the costs, if any, of the project?

5. What happens if one person is not doing a fair share of the work?

6. Who is going to settle disputes?

HOW TO FIND AN EXPERT

Some people know a little about a lot of different things. Experts know a lot about a few things. Nobody knows everything about everything. Where can you find someone who knows about the things you need to know? Your parents may have some great ideas or scientific knowledge, or they may know people in the scientific or business community

Scanning electron microscope in lab at the University of British Columbia, Canada.

who can also give you advice.

You'd be surprised how eager most scientists are to spare a few minutes for an inquiring young mind. The university or college in your area can probably put you in touch with an instructor who may be able to help you solve your problems. You can telephone or write away to universities, labs, or other research facilities and ask for help on specific questions. You can go to the Internet and ask on the science fair help lines. Post your question and there will no doubt be someone who can answer it.

Photomicrograph of dandelion head

How to Write a Letter Asking for Help

When you write away for help or information, the letter should contain the following:
1. Who you are: your full name and grade, as well as the name of your school and teacher. Include your complete mailing address as well as phone number and fax or e-mail address if you have one.
2. Explain why you are contacting this person. Be as specific and detailed as possible.
3. State what you want to know and when you need to know it.
4. Use polite, businesslike language. Thank the person for his or her time and trouble. Have an adult proofread the letter for you before you send it. Use your neatest writing and address the envelope carefully.
5. If the person lives close to you, you may want to ask him or her for an interview, either in person or on the telephone.
6. If you get help, be sure to follow up the assistance with a thank-you note.

Free Stuff

You may be surprised how much information is out there, and it's free for the asking. For example, if you were researching the way that sewage gets treated, you could contact the municipal treatment center. It may run tours or have free pamphlets. If you were looking at electricity, you could write to your local power company and ask for any information on their technology. Many government agencies are wonderful sources of information. National parks and other attractions also often have good reference materials.

Model of a cell.

TYPES OF PROJECTS

There are various kinds of projects you could do. Here are some of them:

Collections: Collections are a group of related objects; for example, a leaf collection or a rock collection. These are usually acceptable for primary or elementary school fairs but not for older students.

A rock collection.

Demonstrations: A demonstration project is a display of a device or something that is already known; for example, an electric motor or the effect of color on heat absorption. Demonstrations are acceptable for younger students but should be avoided by older students.

Experiments: Experiments are investigations in which you test a hypothesis. Most of the projects in this book are experiments. These are suitable for all age and grade levels.

Studies: A study involves collecting data to find a pattern or relationship. Students often use studies for science fair projects. Surveys are one type of study. Measuring the amount of rainfall and measuring the acidity of rainwater are studies.

Inventions: Inventions include designing and developing new devices, models or techniques, or improving old ones. Making a better mousetrap is an example of an invention.

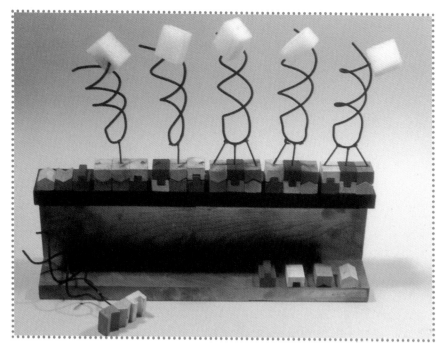
Model of protein synthesis.

THE SCIENTIFIC METHOD

In a science fair project, everything must be measured exactly and accurately described. There is an order to performing a scientific experiment. The first step, once you have chosen a topic or area of study, is to research the topic. This will allow you to narrow your focus to a single problem. Once you have chosen the problem to study, you will need to do additional research to see what approaches other people have taken to the same problem. You will also need to develop a hypothesis to test. The next step is to design your experiment so that you will be able to get reliable results. Then you can perform the experiment and make observations. Finally, when you have completed the experimenting, you can draw some conclusions. Let's look at each of these steps in more detail.

Keep a Journal

Right from the start, you'll need a journal to record your studies and findings. A journal

is a diary for your science experiment. Write down everything of importance, from the first visit to the library to the finished report. Keep a record of all the sources of your information, including books, magazines, encyclopedias, Internet sites, and interviews. This is also where you will describe the proposed experiments and record the raw data you collect.

It is much more important for the journal to be complete and accurate than it is for it to look good. Record important dates and times. This is to be a permanent record of what you did, so you should use a bound notebook, not a looseleaf, and you may wish to write in ink rather than pencil. If you make a mistake, don't use correction fluid or erase it. Just draw a neat line through the error.

Research

One of the best places to begin doing a science fair project is your local or school library. Your librarian is a valuable resource person who can help you find materials and suggest other sources. Reference books such as encyclopedias should be accurate if they contain recent material, but may lack the detail you need. Books, magazines, and newspapers are also available at the library.

For higher level projects you may need to use the library of your local college or university. Call first to find out if students your age are allowed to use the library materials. You may be able to photocopy materials that don't circulate.

Information for your project may come from something you saw on television. Make a note of the program and the time at which you watched it. If possible, watch the listings to see if it is on at a different time and watch the program again, taking notes, or videotape the program. Science programs are usually pretty reliable sources of information, but your memory might not be. Sometimes TV shows have a Web site that you can look at, or even have a monthly magazine featuring articles on the TV shows. You may be able to rent or purchase videos about the show you watched.

If you have access to the Internet, you will be able to find information about most science topics. There are science fair groups that you can access. Remember not to give out any personal information over the Internet. Information on the Internet is not screened for accuracy. Anyone can post information on the Internet, so

don't rely on it without checking other sources.

Interviews are a good way to obtain specific information about your topic. Ask a knowledgeable person or an expert the questions you have. Record the answers, and include this person in your list of sources.

Topic or Problem

Once you have completed your research, you should have a good idea about what problem you will study. After you have learned a little bit about your topic, you should begin to have some questions. The problem gives you the starting point for your project. Try not to continuously change your problem as you

do your research. A problem may be something like "What is the effect of acid rain on seedlings?" or "Which cereal stays crisp the longest in milk?" or "Why do you see fewer stars in the city than in the country?" The problem should be one which can be solved experimentally. It usually is better if the problem is open-ended, not a question for which you can give a simple *yes* or *no* answer.

Hypothesis

A hypothesis is an educated guess based on your research and your own knowledge. It should be a statement that your experiments will allow you to test. It should not begin, "I think that..." or "I believe that...." Instead, simply state what you think the relationship is between the things you are testing. For example: "Acid rain slows the growth of bean seedlings." The hypothesis for your project needs to be specific to the actual experiment you perform. In this book, there is a sample hypothesis for each project given, but we encourage you to plan your own experiments and write your own unique hypothesis to reflect your experiments. The ideas listed under ELEMENTARY LEVEL and JUNIOR HIGH LEVEL give you some more paths to investigate.

Observation

Data are the pieces of information you collect when you perform your experiment. Learn to use any measuring devices correctly and record the values you measure accurately in your journal. Whatever you see when you do the experiment is what you ought to report. Try to be objective when reporting your observations. Make any measurements such as length, weight, or temperature carefully and record them in your journal right away. You should use the metric system for measurements, because that is the system scientists usually use. You may need to use some school equipment to measure things accurately. Check with your teacher.

Experiment

The reason you do the experiment is to test your hypothesis. You need to design the actual experiment. You have to figure out what you need, what you are going to do, and how you are going to do it. You must

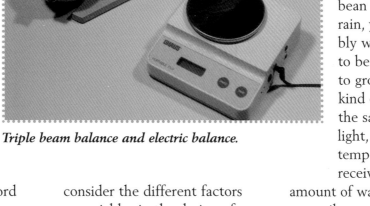

Triple beam balance and electric balance.

consider the different factors or variables in the design of your experiment. The word "variable" means "something that can change." In your experiment, you will need to look at three types of variables: controlled, manipulated, and dependent or responding variables.

The controlled variables are all the conditions in the experiment that you keep the same for all of the samples you test. For example, in an experiment on the growth of bean seedlings in acid rain, you would probably want all the plants to be of the same age, to grow in the same kind of soil, to receive the same amount of light, to be at the same temperature, and to receive the same amount of water. The plants' age, soil, amount of light, temperature, and amount of water are all controlled variables in this experiment. The manipulated variable is what you are

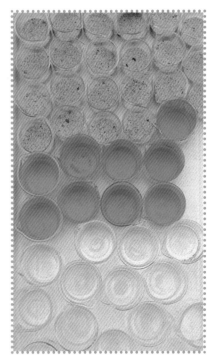

changing in each experiment. You usually have only one manipulated variable in your experiment. In our example on the growth of bean seedlings in acid rain, the manipulated variable is the amount of acid in the water used. The responding variable might be the height of the bean seedling or the number of leaves it has. It is something that you are hoping will change as a result of a change in the manipulated variable. You may have more than one responding variable.

Control

Most experiments require the use of a control. A control is a sample that you treat the same as your experimental samples, except you don't expose it to the manipulated variable. In our bean example, the controls are the seedlings that are watered with plain rainwater, without any acid. The purpose of a control is to allow you to compare the effects of your test to the effects of normal circumstances. If you don't know how the seedlings grow normally, you won't know if they grew any differently when exposed to acid rain.

Repeatability

One of the most important things about an experiment is that you or anyone else must be able to repeat the experiment and get the same results. To test this, you will need to repeat the experiment several times, or with several samples. There is always some variation in experimental results, simply because you can't control everything. Also, measurements that you make are never completely accurate. The devices you use to measure aren't perfect. Repeating the experiment allows you to have a large enough sample size to be able to show a difference if one exists, a difference that is significant and is due to something other than measurement errors or minor variations.

Results and Conclusion

The conclusion summarizes your research and experimental results. Sometimes it agrees with your hypothesis and sometimes it may not. If your results support your hypothesis, say so, and suggest ideas for further experiments. If your results don't support your hypothesis, you need to say that as well. Another experiment or set of experiments may be needed to find out why. While it is tempting to leave out results that don't support your hypothesis, it is dishonest; don't do it. Instead, explain why you think you got the results you did.

Let's say that you have worked really hard, conducted all your research, and did the experiment to the best of your ability, but whatever you thought was going to happen didn't, or whatever you made didn't do what it was supposed to. Now what? Report your findings honestly. Never fake your results. You can learn just as much from an experiment that didn't work as you can from one that did. That's the basic nature of experimentation. You can plan another experiment to try to solve the question you are studying in another way. Scientists build on the studies of other scientists, so the total amount of knowledge people have grows. Fibbing about results is leading people on a false trail, as well as cheating yourself.

There are many examples of science experiments that went "wrong" and produced unexpected good results. There is even a word for this: serendipity, finding something pleasant you weren't looking for. This happened to some famous people:

1. Charles Goodyear accidentally heated some rubber and sulphur on top of a stove and discovered that the rubber stayed flexible and would not burn.

2. Edouard Benedictus discovered safety glass when a glass flask containing a thin film of plastic collodion fell to the ground in his laboratory and cracked, but stayed together.

3. DuPont chemist Julian Hill discovered nylon when he was playing around with fibers in the laboratory.

4. Sir Alexander Fleming discovered penicillin when he noticed that a bit of mold that had fallen into a petri dish he was working on killed bacteria.

TABLES, GRAPHS, AND CHARTS

A picture may not be worth a thousand words, but if you have many pieces of data, a table, graph, or chart is a necessity. People looking at your results should be able to see what you've done without spending hours sifting through your data. Visually presenting your data may help you to see a trend or relationship that you don't see by looking at written numbers alone. A table listing the conditions of the experiment and your results is the quickest way to show your data.

When there appears to be a relationship between the manipulated and responding variables, you can use a line graph. Use a computer to draw it, or draw it by hand on a piece of graph paper. The manipulated variable is always shown across the bottom of the graph on the horizontal (x) axis. The responding variable is shown along the left-hand edge, the vertical (y) axis. Make sure that the numbers on your axes are spaced so they will handle all the pieces of data you collected. Mark the location of your points on the graph carefully and connect them with a line or smooth curve, whichever fits the most points. Graphing can get complicated. You may want to ask a math teacher for help in graphing your results.

Depending on the type of data you collect, you may find it clearer to make a bar graph or a pie chart, used for data where the samples are not sequential. For example, if you did a survey to see which fruit students prefer in their lunches, you could show on a bar graph what numbers of students preferred bananas, oranges, or apples.

VINEGAR AND BEAN SEEDLING HEIGHT

height in cm

mL of vinegar added to water used daily to water beans

MOST POPULAR LUNCH DRINKS

milk
apple juice
tomato juice
soda pop

SURVEY OF STUDENTS' LUNCHBOX FRUIT

Fruit	Number
apples	15
pears	3
oranges	14
bananas	12
grapefruit	1
grapes	7

SURVEY OF STUDENTS' LUNCHBOX FRUIT

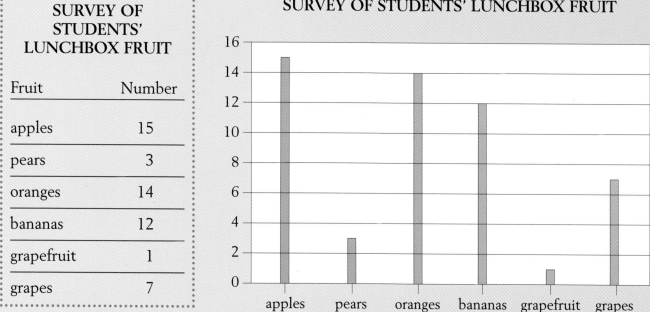

apples   pears   oranges   bananas   grapefruit   grapes

HOW TO WRITE A REPORT

If your science fair requires it, you may need to prepare a separate written report. This report should be neatly written or typed and double-spaced. Include carefully drawn graphs and illustrations or photographs. Put the report in a clearly labeled binder or folder so that judges and visitors to your display can look at it if you are not at the display. A report should include some or all of the following sections.

Title and Title Page

Choose a catchy title that describes your project. The title should be interesting and grab the judges' attention. At the same time it must be appropriate for the project. Think of several different titles and ask your parents, teacher, and your friends which one they prefer. Some fairs require your name, address, school, and grade to be included on the title page; other fairs require only the project title. Check with your teacher to see how information should be presented on the title page.

Table of Contents

The table of contents is a list of the sections of your report. The page number of the first page of each section is also included.

Here is a sample table of contents.

Abstract
Introduction
Experiment
Results and Discussion
Conclusion
Acknowledgments
References

Abstract

An abstract is a project summary. You should briefly describe your problem, the experiments you performed, your data, and conclusion. It is not necessary to go into detail in the abstract, but it is important that it give the judges a taste of your results. For some fairs, the abstract is included as part of your report; in other fairs, the abstract is kept separate. You will probably find it easier to write the abstract after you have completed the rest of your report. Make several copies of the abstract to hand out to people who would like information about your project at the fair.

Introduction

The introduction sets the stage for the rest of the report. This is where you discuss the background information you collected and your reasons for choosing the project.

Experiment

Describe in detail the experiment you performed. Give enough information so another person could repeat or redo

your project. Give information about the materials you used and what you did with them. Be sure to indicate any and all variables that you controlled in your experiment. You may wish to include photographs or drawings of your materials if they are not suitable for display at the fair.

Results and Discussion

This is the most important part of your report. Your results should be described and discussed thoroughly. If possible, the values you obtained should be compared to those found in similar experiments from your research. Make sure your readers can see the connection between your data and your conclusions clearly. Discuss any possible sources of errors. Don't blame anyone for the errors, if any. (NOT: "My little brother kept opening the freezer.") Instead, describe the error. ("Temperature changes occurred during measurement because the freezer door was opened.") Describe any differences you observed among the repeated trials of your experiment. Discuss what you could have done differently and what you would like to do next time to continue the study.

Conclusion

This is a brief summary of your results. You are essentially sum-marizing the most important results from your discussion.

Acknowledgments

Even though you did the actual project yourself, you probably had some help. This is where you thank people, businesses, groups, and schools who assisted you. Normally, you name them, thank them, and describe briefly what kind of assistance they gave you.

References

When doing research, you need to record your sources of information. List them alphabetically in the references section by the authors' last names. Include people you interviewed. Use the following reference formats.

Book: Name of author, book title, name of publisher, city of publication, copyright date, and page numbers.
Magazine or Periodical: Name of author, title of article, title of magazine, volume number, date of publication, page numbers.
Newspaper: Name of author, title of article, name of newspaper, date of publication, section and page numbers.
Encyclopedia: Title of article, name of encyclopedia, volume number, name of publisher, city of publication, copyright date and page numbers.

CD-ROM Encyclopedia or Software Program: Name of program, release number or version, name and location of software company.
Documents from the Internet or Online Services: Name of author if given, title of document, name of posting organization, location of posting organization, date of document, online address or mailing address where the document can be obtained.
Personal Interview: Name of person interviewed, any professional titles or degrees (such as Ph.D., M.D.), address, and phone number.

CHECKING YOUR SPELLING

If you are using a computer for the written part of your report, make sure you run a spelling check of all the words. Nothing detracts from a written report more than silly spelling errors. Have an adult read the report for grammar and syntax. Avoid slang in your written report.

THE DISPLAY

Your display does more than tell the judges what you did; it's also your way of showing them that your project is the best! With a little creativity and care, your display can wow the judges and impress your classmates.

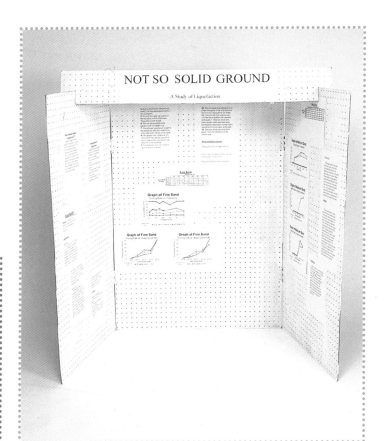

Traditional backboard from the front, showing display.

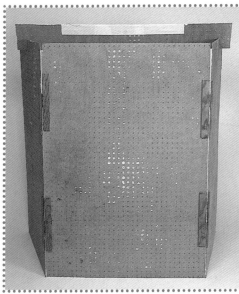

Traditional backboard, seen from the back, showing hinges.

The Backboard

Traditional Method of Making a Backboard

For many science fairs, display backboards must be a certain size, which may not be the same as any materials you have around the house. For competition, displays usually have a back panel 34" wide × 48" tall (86 cm × 122 cm), and two side panels 28" wide × 48" tall (71 cm × 122 cm). Check the dimensions with your teacher, as they can vary from region to region. The backboard should be made of sturdy materials, so that it won't fall over. It must be able to support your report and other information about the project. It must not be flammable. The display can be cut from a single sheet of plywood 4 ft × 8 ft (1.2 m × 2.4 m). Paint the wood with nonleaded paint.

Some fairs will not allow corrugated cardboard, Bristol board, or other flimsy paper products for backboards; check with your teacher. You may use colorful cardboard pasted over the backboard for decoration.

You may need an adult's assistance to assemble the backboard. Attach the boards together with hinges. The board must be able to stand erect without tipping or being nailed to a wall. Make the display easy to assemble and take apart.

Try This Instead

At many lumber stores, hardware stores, and sign and display companies, there is a plastic product used for commercial display purposes. It comes in many different colors and looks like two flat pieces of plastic with a corrugated inside, similar to corrugated cardboard. This product is sometimes called Choroplast. This stuff makes the perfect material for science fair displays. The store may even cut it to match the regulation-sized display, and it will leave you with an extra piece for the title. Refer to the previous section for sizes to cut.

Once the plastic board is cut to size, simply create a hinge using duct tape on the back side of the board.

Display of cut Choroplast; hinged at back with duct tape.

Because it is colored, you don't have to worry about creating an eye-catching background. Because it is plastic, it won't rip if you have to remove any papers from the display, and it never needs painting. Using this display actually saves time and money, and you can reuse this year after year. It is light enough for even a young child to carry to school. Using this material is much easier than creating a heavy wooden display.

Another Possibility

Many stationery stores and science supply companies sell inexpensive regulation-sized science fair boards. These are usually white and need some decorating, but they work

Backboard of Choroplast that has been cut, finished at front, and set up.

well in a pinch.

The photos of some actual displays shown on page 26 give you some idea of how displays can be organized.

How To Put It All Together

Ask your teacher if there are any rules regarding the placement of materials on the board. Usually the title of the project is placed at the top of the center panel. The title should be large enough to be read from at least 4 feet (1.2 m) away. Be sure the various parts of your experiment — purpose, hypothesis, research, proce-

Some displays.

dure, results, and conclusion — are clearly and attractively displayed. Follow the rules for your particular fair as to the placement of the parts on your display. Your display should be neat, in a logical order, and easy to read and understand.

The Display Table and Signs

You might cover the table with fabric or colored paper. Arrange your report, journal, abstract, and other relevant and interesting materials. The key here is to make it pretty. If you have access to a computer, use it. Everything should be printed neatly and mounted to the backboard in an attractive manner. Don't glue or tape any materials to the backboard until you are sure that's where you want them. Lay out all the materials. Ask for someone else's opinion before attaching them to the backboard.

You may love fancy, artistic lettering, but it may be difficult for the judges to read. It is better to use a clear, bold type face or lettering style which will stand out and be easily seen.

Spares

Things break, fall apart, get lost, or get crinkled. Have an emergency kit containing all sorts of supplies you might need in case anything goes wrong on the day of the fair.

TRACING THE STARS

TRACING THE STARS

Tracing the Stars

TRACING THE STARS

TRACING THE STARS

Smoke and Mirrors

At science fairs, the person who has the most toys sometimes wins. Students who have access to video recorders, scanners, high tech computer graphics programs, color printers, and laptop computers can influence judging by creating eye-catching displays. You don't need to own all these gadgets. Many schools have computers that you can borrow. There are businesses in every city which offer color printing and photocopying services, and you can rent a portable computer for a day. If you don't own a camera, you could buy a disposable one. They are inexpensive and take very good pictures, which can be used as part of your display.

Having said all that, let's note that it's not necessary to do any of it. Your science fair project should be based on sound scientific research and clear and insightful writing. You don't need the whistles and bells if you have done your best work.

Display Considerations

Although some of the items below may have been used as part of your project, you may not use them on your display table. Check the regulations of the fair carefully to make sure your display complies. Here are some of the more commonly restricted items:

▶ No live organisms. Plants may or may not be alright, depending on the fair. No fish, no hamsters, no birds, no creepy crawly things, no animals of any sort.

▶ Nothing wet: no water, no juices, no vinegar, no taste-testing. No dry ice or other sublimating solids.

▶ Nothing that burns. No open flames, either.

▶ Batteries are alright, but not if they are opened.

▶ No chemicals. No aerosols. No gases. No sprays. No household cleaners.

▶ Nothing dangerous. No guns, ammunition, or other weapons of any sort.

▶ No drugs or controlled substances. No poisons.

▶ Nothing sharp, including knives, syringes, or scissors.

▶ No body parts, except for hair, teeth, nails, and cleaned, dried bones.

▶ Nothing cultured, including fungi and bacteria.

▶ If you are using volunteer models who are not members of your family, have them sign release forms, which permit you to use their photos at the science fair.

If you used any of the above things in your project, it's not a problem unless the fair specifically excludes it, such as an experiment with animals. You can make a display for your project by taking a photo or using a video camera. If you have photos, you can scan them into a computer and print them out on paper.

Good and Bad Displays

A good display is well organized, colorful, and inviting to look at. It may appeal to people's curiosity with its title and displays. On page 29 are two drawings of displays of the same project. Which do you think is better and why? How could the one on the right be improved?

THE ORAL PRESENTATION

It's not enough to have done a great project and display. Most schools require an oral presentation as part of the science fair. The judges and your teacher will go from display to display and ask each student to discuss his or her project. Here's what you need to do:

1. Prior to the fair, review all your material and prepare cue cards to cover the main points you want to tell the judges about during the fair.

2. Practice with a friend or family member, so you feel comfortable with the information.

Two displays.

3. Get your family and friends to ask you questions about the project you have done, as the judges will do at the fair.

4. Be prepared for unusual or hard questions. Some judges ask where you got your idea from or where you did your research. Some even ask what you would do differently if you had to do it over again.

5. Don't worry if you don't know the answer to a question. It is better to say, "I didn't come across the answer to that question in my background research" than it is to guess or to say, "I don't know."

6. Look at the judges directly. Try not to stare at your feet. Be confident.

GOOD MANNERS

▶ Science fair judging can take a long time, depending on the number of judges and the number of students participating. It can be a long day. Take something to keep you amused, such as a book, hand-held video game, or portable disk or tape player. Do not disturb the other students.

▶ It is inappropriate and rude to make fun of someone else's science fair project, but feel free to discuss projects with the other students and talk about your project. It will help you get over the jitters when speaking to the judges. Take interest in other students' work; you may learn something new and interesting from their science fair projects.

▶ No horseplay. You may accidentally knock over someone's display. Talk quietly among yourselves.

▶ Never touch another student's display or remove any items from someone else's table!

7. Wear clean clothes that are neat and tidy.

8. It's advisable to clean up your language. No swear words, of course. Avoid the words "like" and "right" and "OK" at the beginning and end of each sentence. NO: "OK ... Like, I gathered the information from the Internet, right?" YES: "I used the Internet for part of my research."

9. If you are showing a videotape of your experiment or using a computer as part of your demonstration, make certain that you know how everything operates before you try this at the fair. Also, make sure you did the work on the computer, as the judges will ask you how you got the information into the computer.

WHAT DO THE JUDGES LOOK FOR?

Usually, some basic guidelines are given to judges. Each school and region may have its own rules. Most fairs look for some or all of the following:

1. Project Design

▶ Is this an original project?

▶ Has the problem been clearly identified?

▶ Have you controlled the necessary variables?

▶ Has background research been done thoroughly?

2. Acquired Skills

▶ Do you have the skills to have done the project without assistance?

▶ Do you understand how the equipment was used?

3. Project Data

▶ Was a journal used to record your data?

▶ Were the experiments repeated several times?

▶ How much time was spent on the project?

4. Conclusion

▶ Were the data organized into appropriate tables, charts, and graphs?

▶ Were data explained using appropriate language and research?

▶ Were sufficient data collected to support conclusions?

▶ Were conclusions made using the data collected?

5. Presentation

▶ Did you prepare a complete report?

▶ Were you able to answer questions about the project?

▶ Did you use the display when discussing the project?

▶ Was the display attractive and well organized?

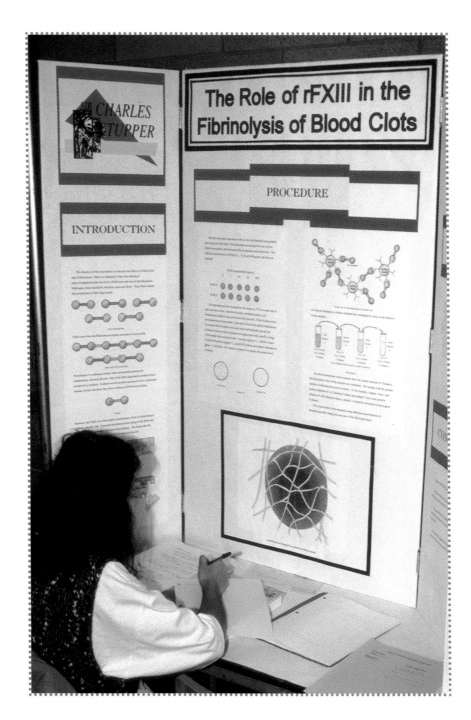

SAFETY FIRST

Before you start any projects, there are a few safety do's and don'ts to keep in mind.

Do's

1. Ask an adult before handling any materials, foods, chemicals, or equipment.

2. Have an adult handle all sharp objects such as knives or razor blades and help you with appliances such as blenders and stoves if you don't usually operate these yourself.

3. Wash your hands after doing the experiments.

4. Tie back long hair while you work, and avoid wearing clothing with long, loose sleeves, which could knock things over.

5. Keep your work area clean, and clean up any spills immediately.

6. Plan your project carefully to be sure that you know what you are going to do before you begin experimenting, and assemble your supplies.

7. Always work in a well-ventilated area with adequate lighting.

8. Tell an adult immediately if you hurt yourself in any way.

9. Keep all supplies, tools, chemicals, and experiments out of the reach of very young children.

10. Check safety and disposal instructions with your teacher or a supplier before using any chemicals.

Don'ts

1. If you are allergic to or sensitive to any foods or other substances, do not use them to perform experiments.

2. Do not taste, eat, or drink any of the experiments.

3. Do not kill or be cruel to any living creatures in your experiments.

CHEMICAL SAFETY

Here are some of the sources you can check to learn more about the safe handling of the chemicals you might use in your project:

*Material Safety Data Sheets (MSDS): Available from the chemical supplier and should be included in the packaging materials for any chemicals purchased. Your school should have these available for any chemicals it allows you to use.

Chemical Rubber Company (CRC) Handbook: Gives a listing of most chemicals and their physical and chemical properties. CRC Handbooks are updated annually and are available in most libraries.

*Safety in Academic Chemistry Laboratories: Available from the American Chemical Society, Career Publications, 1155 16th St. N. W., Washington, D.C. 20036

Nothing to Sneeze At

When people tell you to cover your mouth when you cough or sneeze, they are trying to teach you more than good manners; they are trying to protect others around you from breathing in your germs. When you sneeze, the microorganisms move outwards from your mouth and nose in all directions. Here is a way to simulate this movement, using a bursting balloon. This experiment will give you an idea of how covering your mouth may affect how far the airborne germs travel.

PURPOSE: To build a model to demonstrate how far airborne germs travel.
HYPOTHESIS: A barrier limits the movement of airborne particles like germs.

Materials
▶ tire pump
▶ large balloon
▶ confetti
▶ piece of writing paper
▶ pin
▶ chalk
▶ tape measure
▶ large piece of cardboard

Research Sources
▶ biology teacher
▶ virologist
▶ epidemiologist
▶ Related topics: infectious diseases, infection, pathogens, viruses, bacteria, mycoplasms, disease

Procedure

1. Place a measured handful of confetti in a deflated balloon. Use a funnel to help you get all the tiny pieces into the mouth of the balloon.
2. Use a tire pump to blow up the balloon. (This will keep the confetti from getting too wet.)
3. Inflate the balloon as full as possible without popping.
4. Stand on a piece of paper in the middle of a large room. Mark the place you stand with a pencil. The place you stand is the zero distance for your measurements. Mark circles of diameter 1 foot (30 cm), 2 feet (60 cm), 3 feet (94 cm) and 4 feet (122 cm) with chalk, measuring outward, with the place you stood as the center.
5. Return to your central standing place and pop the balloon with a pin.
6. Count the number of confetti pieces that fell inside a circle of radius 1 foot (30 cm) from your zero point. Next count the pieces of confetti that are within a circle of radius 2 feet (60 cm). Move outwards in 1 foot (30 cm) intervals, counting the number in each circle. Record your findings on a table.
7. Do the experiment again, this time holding a large piece of cardboard in front of the balloon before you pop it. Count the pieces of confetti in each circle from your zero point again.

Results

How many pieces of confetti fell in each circle? Where did the most confetti land? Were the pieces of confetti evenly distributed? What effect did the cardboard have on the confetti distribution? How do you think this is similar to the passage of germs through the air?

Display Hints

Display a photograph of the room with the confetti on the floor.

Draw a line graph showing the radius of each circle and the average number of pieces of confetti in each.

GOING FURTHER

Elementary Level

What are some ways that germs or diseases can be spread?

How do antibacterial soaps work? How effective are they? Survey your classmates to see who uses them and who doesn't and how many colds each group had last winter.

Junior High Level

How can you protect yourself from viruses and bacteria? Try growing some safe bacteria on an agar plate, such as yogurt bacteria. Ask your teacher what types of safe bacteria are available for you to work with. What types of bacteria are normally found on your skin? What materials can be used to stop their growth?

Genetic Printing

Do you look like one of your parents? Do you have your mother's eyes and your father's lips? Well ... give them back. Your eyes, your hair color, and even your body structure may resemble those of a parent or grandparent, but how about some of the things which aren't so obvious, like your fingerprints? People have unique finger-prints, which is why they can be used as a form of identification. Different shapes which make up the fingerprint allow you to categorize them. Do your family members have common shapes in their finger-prints? Here is a way to check.

PURPOSE: To determine if members of the same family have any fingerprint character-istics in common.

HYPOTHESIS: Members of the same family have fingerprints that are more similar than those of unrelated individuals.

Materials
▶ magnifying glass
▶ paper
▶ stamp pad with ink

Research Sources
▶ police and fingerprinting experts
▶ geneticists
▶ books or magazine articles on detective or forensic science
▶ Related topics: genetics, identification, skin, epider-mis, dermis

Procedure
1. Make a list of volunteers and their family members from several families who are willing to participate in the experi-ment; the more, the better. For each volunteer, take a finger-print of the right index finger by rolling the tip of the finger on an ink pad, then rolling it on a clean sheet of paper. Use a separate sheet of paper for each person. Assign each per-son a random number, and label each print with the same number, so that no one except you knows which fingerprint

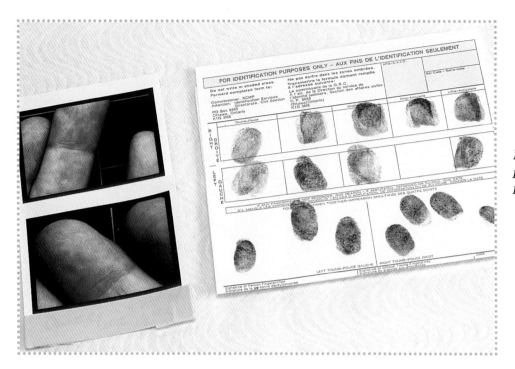

Police form with finger-prints. At left, enlarged photo of fingerprints.

belongs to which person. Make sure you keep an accurate record of which print comes from which person. Get prints from members of a large number of families.

2. When you have finished collecting the prints, use a magnifying glass to take a close look at the fingerprints from each person and try to categorize the prints. Keep a record of your findings in your notebook. Consult your references, including the diagram in this project, so you can correctly describe the types of shapes in each print.

3. Study your findings and see if the members of each family have fingerprints with any common shapes.

Fingerprint shapes.

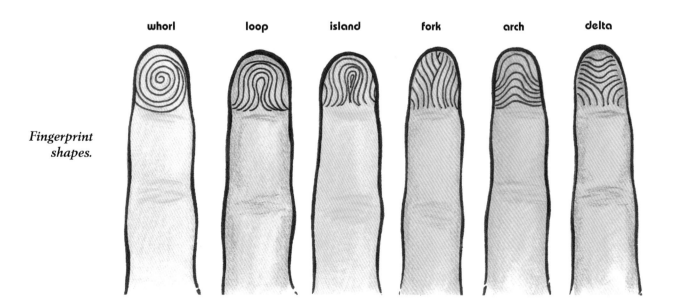

whorl   loop   island   fork   arch   delta

4. Set up a bulletin board with the prints (still unidentified by family) randomly placed on the board. Ask volunteers to see if they can group the prints by family. Ask each volunteer to write down the groupings he or she finds. For example: "Numbers 1, 5, 8 are from one family and Numbers 2, 7, 9 are one family."

5. Study your volunteers' results and see how successful they were in grouping the prints by family.

Results

What shapes were seen in the fingerprints you observed? Did people find similar patterns of whorls, loops, etc., in members of the same family groups?

Display Hints

Display family members' prints grouped and the similarities, if any, circled. Include sketches or samples of the different shapes in fingerprints. Have paper and an ink pad ready so that visitors to your display can be printed if they wish.

GOING FURTHER

Elementary Level

Make prints of some volunteers' left-hand fingers and right-hand fingers. See if there are any common features. Ask people in your class if they can match the correct left-hand prints with the right-hand prints of the same person. Make a family tree of eye color in several families.

Junior High Level

How common is each type of shape seen in fingerprints? Are the shapes seen on toes the same as the ones on fingers? Trace the pattern of several features through several families to see if you can tell which are inherited and which are acquired.

Got Milk?

You may have heard that drinking milk helps you grow strong bones and teeth. It turns out that what makes your bones strong is the calcium in the milk. All bones contain calcium, including your bones and a chicken's bones. (Chickens get calcium from grains.) What would happen if we took the calcium away? Here is a way to model the effect of the loss of calcium in bones. We will use vinegar, an acid, which dissolves the calcium in bones.

PURPOSE: To examine the effect of the loss of calcium on bone strength.

HYPOTHESIS: When calcium is added to bones in vinegar, the amount of calcium dissolved out of the bones is less, and the bones bend less, than bones in vinegar alone.

Materials

- 6 or more chicken bones, all about the same size, from cooked chicken(s)
- 6 or more glass jars
- measuring cup
- vinegar
- calcium tablets or drops
- plastic wrap
- postage scale or other accurate scale
- labels

Research Sources

- nutritionist or dietician
- science or biology teacher
- public health agencies
- books on diet and nutrition
- health pamphlets, available from doctors or pharmacists
- Related topics: osteoclasts, parathyroid gland, bone formation, calcium phosphate, vitamin D, calcification

Procedure

Note: Bacteria can grow on chicken, so be sure to wash up your hands and work surfaces with hot, soapy water after working on your project.

1. Carefully clean off any chicken meat from the bones and dispose of it. Choose bones as close to each other in size as possible and examine them carefully. Weigh them to check that they are

Chicken bones in vinegar.

take pictures of the bones, feel them, and note any softness or flexibility each day. Record your findings.

Results

What happened when the vinegar was first added to the jars? What happened to the bone in water only? How did the bones that were in vinegar only change each day? Was there a difference between the bones with and without calcium? Did the amount of calcium added make a difference in bone flexibility?

Display Hints

Display photographs and sketches of the bones. Include a table showing contents of the different jars and your daily observations. Dry and display some of the bones you used in the experiment.

close in weight. Sketch or take pictures of the bones, feel them, and note how bendable they are and any softness.

2. Place each bone in a separate glass jar and label the jar.

3. Take one jar with a bone in it and fill it with water. This is your control.

4. Pour an equal amount of vinegar into each of the remaining jars. Make sure that the vinegar completely covers the bone. If necessary, add an equal amount of additional vinegar to each jar to cover the bone.

5. Set 3 of the jars aside. They will have vinegar and bones only. Add different amounts of calcium tablets or drops to each of the remaining jars, perhaps starting with one-half tablet and increasing to 5

tablets. Note the contents of each jar on its label.

6. Cover the jars with plastic wrap to seal. Put them in a warm place where they won't be disturbed. Check them once a day for 4 or 5 days. Sketch or

GOING FURTHER

Elementary Level

Eggshells also contain calcium. Try this experiment with eggshells instead of chicken bones.

Junior High Level

Remove the bones and evaporate the liquid in the jars. Look at what remains (the residue) in each jar with a microscope or magnifying glass. How does the residue in the jars with calcium tablets added compare to the residue in the jar containing vinegar without calcium? Repeat the same experiment using a carbonated drink instead of vinegar.

Scents of Smell

Many stores offer aromatherapy products. These essential oils are supposed to make you feel a certain way after you smell them, but do they really work?

PURPOSE: To determine if different aromas make you feel the way they are advertised to do on the bottle.

HYPOTHESIS: People respond differently when asked to describe the feelings evoked by essential oils _____, _____, _____ (fill in the names of the ones you use).

Materials

▶ bottles of several different essential oils or essences with the aromatherapy claims (advertisements) that they are sold with

▶ 35 mm film canister and its cover for each oil

▶ cotton ball for each oil

▶ eyedropper

▶ labels

▶ pen

▶ coffee beans

Research Sources

▶ biology books or books on the sense of smell

▶ books, pamphlets, or magazine articles on aromatherapy

▶ psychology books

▶ aromatherapist

▶ psychologist or medical doctor

▶ Related topics: pheromones, smell, senses, emotion, placebo effect, chemo-receptors

Procedure

1. Buy several essential oils or essences from a store. Be sure each essence or oil has a label or information sheet describing how the odor is supposed to make people feel. Choose several different oils, including ones that promise to make you feel calm, relaxed, alert, etc.; for example, musk, eucalyptus, peppermint, rose.

samples, the volunteer should smell the coffee beans to clear out the previous odor.

6. After all the volunteers have completed the experiment, collect the papers and examine your results.

Results
Did the volunteers agree on their responses to any of the oils? Was there any relationship between the way the volunteers responded and the way the oil was advertised to make a person feel?

Display Hints
Display different bottles with the manufacturers' claims of how they will make you feel. Place your film canisters on the display table with scents for the judges to smell. Draw a bar graph showing the results of your survey.

2. Record in your journal how each odor is advertised to make you feel. Place a cotton ball inside each film canister. Put 2 drops of each scent on the cotton ball with the dropper and seal the canister with its lid. Assign each canister a number and label on the outside with the number alone so that no one knows what is inside the canister. Make up a chart that lists the ways the various odors could make you feel, include the advertised feeling and some others that aren't advertised.

3. Put some coffee beans in a canister also, and close it.

4. Conduct a test using a large number of volunteers. A school class is a good-sized sample of people, if your teacher allows the students in your class to participate. Hand each student or volunteer a sheet with the

table to fill out during the experiment.

5. Have each volunteer open a canister and smell the odor of the oil or essence inside; then he or she should check off the boxes on the table that most accurately describe how the odor makes the volunteer feel. The volunteer should repeat this for each canister. Between

GOING FURTHER

Elementary Level
Investigate how your sense of smell works. How much of a substance is needed before someone can smell something? Are certain people better able to detect odors than others?

Junior High Level
People have the ability to identify a huge number of smells. How many can a large group of volunteers identify? Are smell and memory related? Design an experiment to test this.

The Yolk's on You

When you spend a long time in the bathtub, you may notice that your skin begins to wrinkle. This is caused by something called osmosis. Osmosis is the movement of a solvent (such as water) across a membrane separating two solutions of different concentrations. The movement of the solvent is usually in the direction of the solution that has the higher amount of dissolved material. The water in the tub enters the top layer of your skin, which has many dissolved things in the cells, and makes it swell up. The layer of skin underneath stays the same size, so the wrinkles form in the top layer.

An egg is one large cell, and you can use an egg to see how water moves across its membrane. We can do this by measuring the liquid level in the egg. When the level increases, more liquid has entered the egg.

Warning: Raw eggs may contain harmful bacteria. You should always wash your hands and any utensils and surfaces which have touched them after handling raw eggs. Use hot, soapy water.

PURPOSE: To study what affects the liquid levels in eggs.
HYPOTHESIS: When the egg is placed in fresh water, the liquid level in the straw will rise higher than when the egg is placed in salt water.

Materials

▶ small jars
▶ distilled water
▶ fresh raw eggs
▶ egg cups or narrow glasses, such as champagne glass
▶ tweezers
▶ spoon
▶ knife
▶ clear plastic drinking straws
▶ candle
▶ matches
▶ modeling clay
▶ salt
▶ ruler

Research Sources

▶ biology teachers
▶ books and magazines on biology
▶ Related topics: hypotonic, hypertonic and isotonic solutions; osmosis; semi-permeable membrane; osmotic pressure; homeostasis

Procedure

1. Fill a jar to just below the rim with the distilled water.

2. Place the pointed end of the egg in the egg cup or glass. Use a spoon to gently tap the rounded end of the egg to crack the shell. Don't tap too hard, as you don't want to break the egg open.

3. Using tweezers or your fingers, gently peel away a small section of the shell, making sure you leave the rubbery membrane intact.

4. Carefully lift the egg from the egg cup and place it, with the rounded end down, in the glass jar. Have an adult use a knife to cut a small hole in the pointed end of the egg. The hole should be about the same diameter as the straw.

5. Place the straw in the hole so that it goes about halfway into the egg. Put modeling clay around the hole so that it seals the straw to the egg. Leave this setup in a place where it will not be disturbed. Observe every few hours and mark the liquid level on the straw with a pen. Measure the level with the ruler and record your findings in your journal. If possible, photograph your results at several times.

Carefully remove part of the shell with tweezers, without breaking the membrane

Uncovered membrane is in the water. Straw is attached with modeling clay.

6. Repeat the experiment several times, with a new egg each time. Instead of distilled water, use water with salt dissolved in it. For each egg, use a different amount of salt in the water.

Results

What happened to the level of liquid in the straw? What distance up the straw did the liquid travel in each time interval? What happened when you added salt to the water? Did different concentrations of salt in the water change the results?

Display Hints

Display photos of the egg with the straw attached taken at different times during the experiment. Draw a line graph showing the distance the liquid traveled up the straw over time for each salt solution, and draw one for the egg in plain distilled water. Use an egg motif for the border of your written materials.

GOING FURTHER

Elementary Level

Keep a record of how long it takes for the liquid to rise in the straw. Try the experiment in a warm and a cold place. Does the temperature of the room affect the liquid level?

Junior High Level

Does the freshness of the eggs affect the water level? What happens if you replace the salt with sugar?

The Sensitive Plant

Do you talk to your plants? Do you like to touch them? If you touch the leaves of some plants, the edges of the leaves turn brown. One type of plant will actually pull away from you if you touch it — the *Mimosa pudica*. It can be used for a quick project. *Mimosa pudica* is particularly responsive to stimuli. The leaves close very rapidly when you blow on them or touch them. If the plant then is left undisturbed, its leaves quickly return to their open condition. These plants can be purchased at plant specialty stores; they grow wild in some areas. If you have lots of time, you can grow your own *Mimosa pudica* from seed.

▶ PURPOSE: To study how Mimosa pudica plants react to different stimuli.

HYPOTHESIS: *Mimosa pudica* leaves close in response to touch, moving air, cold, and dark.

Materials

- ▶ packet of *Mimosa pudica* seeds* or fully grown *Mimosa pudica* plant
- ▶ peat pots*
- ▶ refrigerator with freezer
- ▶ water*
- ▶ bowl*
- ▶ toothpicks or cotton swabs
- ▶ perfume or vinegar
- ▶ radio or musical instrument
- ▶ plastic bags*
- ▶ ties to close plastic bags*
- ▶ small plant pots, 2 to 3 inches (5 to 7.5 cm) in diameter*
- ▶ potting soil*

Research Sources

- ▶ biology or science teacher
- ▶ books or magazines on botany
- ▶ plant or gardening magazines
- ▶ florist or gardening expert
- ▶ Related topics: plant germination and growth, tropism, thigmotropism, turgor pressure

The starred items are only needed if you grow your own seedlings.

Procedure

If you aren't growing your own seedlings, skip the first part and start at Part Two.

Part One: Grow Your Own Seedlings

1. Place the seed package in your freezer and leave it overnight.
2. Remove the seeds from the freezer and, with an adult's assistance, place the seeds in a cup of boiling water. This should crack the seed coats and allow the seeds to germinate faster.
3. Place the peat pots in a bowl of warm water until they swell.
4. Plant 3 seeds in each peat pot, making sure that they are spaced apart from each other.
5. Place the peat pots in plastic bags and seal with ties. Keep them in a very warm spot (80°F or 30°C). In about 10 days, you should have some seedlings.
6. Transplant seedlings into larger pots with soil when they are about 2 inches (5 cm) tall, and move them somewhere with lots of light. Remember to keep the soil moist.
7. Let them grow until they have several sets of leaves.

Part Two: Sensitivity Project

For each part of the experiment, sketch or photograph the plants, and note the plants' responses in your journal.
1. Use a toothpick or a cotton swab to gently touch a plant. How long does it take the plant to fold or unfold?
2. Gently blow on the plant leaves. Note what happens.
3. Place your plant in the refrigerator for a short time.
4. Place your plant in a covered box for about 2 minutes.

Plant with leaves open.

Plant with leaves closed.

Conditioning Project

Repeat the tests on your plant over several days or weeks. As your plant matures, does it become less sensitive to touch? Experiment with steps you can take to keep your plant moving. Try pruning or cutting back your plant.

Results

What happens when you touch the leaves of the plant? How do the leaves change when exposed to heat, cold, and dark? How can you restore the sensitivity to your plant?

Display Hints

Display several plants for touching. Display your sketches and photos.

GOING FURTHER

Elementary Level

Try some other stimuli, such as perfume, vinegar, and music, to see if the *Mimosa pudica* reacts to them.

Junior High Level

Find some other plants that respond to touch, such as the Sundew (*Drosera*) or Venus' flytrap (*Dionea*), and do some experiments with them.

The Sundew (Drosera) plant has sticky hairs that attract insects, which it then digests.

Which Way Did It Go?

If you have ever grown a bean plant from a seed, you will understand why the story says that Jack grew a beanstalk rather than corn or peas. Beans are one of the fastest-growing plants around, and also are easy seeds to germinate. Just get them wet, warm them up, and in no time they will be growing up into the sky! But just how do plants know what direction to grow in? Plants grow towards light and up away from the soil. The way an organism reacts, by motion or another change, to a specific stimulus, is called a tropism. "Phototropism" refers to a plant's tendency to grow towards light. "Geotropism" means the tendency of the roots to grow down into the soil, and the tendency for the shoots to grow upwards.

PURPOSE: To study the effects of light and gravity on bean seedlings.

HYPOTHESIS: When bean seedlings are lighted from one side, they will grow towards the light. Bean seedlings will grow so their leaves grow up and their roots grow down, regardless of how they are positioned.

Materials
- packet of bean seeds (wax, pole, or scarlet runner beans)
- peat pots
- paper towels
- water
- plastic bags to fit peat pots
- ties for plastic bags
- pots for seedlings, 2 to 3 inches (5 to 7.5 cm) wide
- potting soil
- twine
- coat hanger
- cardboard
- scissors or craft knife
- light

Research Sources
- biology or science teacher
- books or magazine articles on botany

- plant or gardening magazines
- florist or gardening expert
- Related topics: plant germination and growth, geotropism, phototropism, gravitropism, statoliths, auxins

Procedure

Part One: Grow Your Seedlings

1. Remove the seeds from the package and place the seeds in a damp paper towel overnight to allow the seeds to germinate. If necessary, leave them for more time.
2. Place the peat pots in a bowl of warm water until they swell.
3. Plant one seed in each peat pot.
4. Place the peat pots in plastic bags and seal. Keep them in a very warm spot (80°F or 30°C). In about 3 or 4 days, you should have some seedlings.
5. Transplant seedlings into larger pots with soil when they are about 2 inches (5 cm) tall, and move them somewhere with lots of light. Remember to keep the soil moist.

For each part of each experiment, note and sketch the results in your journal. Take photos if you can.

Part Two: Geotropism Experiments

1. Cut a circle of cardboard to cover the top of the plant pot, and cut a slit in it for the stem of the seedling. This will hold the soil in place when it is tipped.
2. Tip the pot on its side.
3. Let the seedling grow in this position, and watch to see what happens.

4. Try turning it in another direction. If you can, turn it upside down. (You can tie it and hang it from a coat hanger.)

Part Three: Phototropism Experiments

1. Place the seedlings in a dimly lit room, or shield the seedlings from the light, using a large piece of cardboard.
2. Shine a light on the plant from one direction and watch as the plant grows towards the light. Leave the plant in this position with the light shining from one side for several days.
3. Change the direction of the light on the plant, and observe the plant for several days.

Results

How does the plant grow when you change its position? What happens when you turn

it upside down? What happens when you change the direction of the light?

Display Hints

Display sketches or photographs of the plants during the various stages of the experiments, showing their responses to the various stimuli.

GOING FURTHER

Elementary Level

Try growing plants near a warm air outlet or a radiator. Are they attracted to the heat? Do different types of bean plants act in the same way when placed near a light source?

Junior High Level

Plant hormones are available at many garden stores; sometimes they are sold as rooting compounds. Find out how to use them and test to see if plants treated with hormones form roots faster than they do without hormones. What different treatments are required to germinate different types of seeds? Is there a pattern in the way seeds must be treated related to their size or the thickness of the seed coat?

Leafy Greens

Make sure you eat your leafy greens. Leafy green plants are full of nutrients you need, and their leaves are the original solar energy collectors. Light from the sun supplies energy for the plants to grow. When there is lots of sunlight, the plant stores the sun's energy in the form of starch. When no light can strike the leaves, the plant breaks down the starch to use as food. You can test for the presence of starch because starch combines with iodine to turn a blue-black color. Here is a project that looks at how the sun's energy is collected and stored.

PURPOSE: To study how light affects leaves.

HYPOTHESIS: The plant leaves that were in the light contain more starch than the plant leaves that were in the dark.

Materials

▶ leafy green plant (geraniums work well)
▶ aluminum foil
▶ rubbing alcohol
▶ at least four 8-oz (250 mL) jars with lids
▶ measuring cup
▶ saucers or shallow dishes
▶ tincture of iodine
▶ labels

Research Sources

▶ biology or science teacher
▶ books or magazine articles on botany or gardening
▶ florist or gardening expert
▶ Related topics: plant growth, photosynthesis, sugar, starch, carbohydrates

Procedure

1. Wrap several leaves in aluminum foil so that no light can get through.

2. Leave the plant in a sunny place for at least two days.

Geranium with some leaves wrapped.

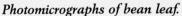

Leaves being tested.

Results

How are the leaves exposed to light different from the leaves kept in the dark? How do plants make starch? What is the starch used for by the plant?

Display Hints

Display sketches or photographs of the leaves. Try preserving the leaves between sheets of wax paper or clear adhesive plastic.

3. Cut off the wrapped leaves and at least 2 leaves that were in the sun.

4. Place about one cup (250 mL) of rubbing alcohol in a jar for each leaf you are testing. Label each jar so that you can tell what conditions the leaf experienced.

5. Drop each leaf into a jar containing alcohol. Close the lids. Leave the jars overnight or for at least 12 hours.

6. Put each leaf on a saucer and drop a few drops of tincture of iodine on the leaf. Note the results for each leaf in your journal. The iodine tells you which leaf made some starch and which did not, because iodine turns blue-black in the presence of starch.

GOING FURTHER

Elementary Level

Test other parts of the plant to see if starch is made in the flowers, stems, or roots. Does the effect of darkness become greater if the plant is covered for a longer time? How much light is needed to make starch? Will a table lamp be enough, or do you have to use sunlight?

Junior High Level

What effects do colored lights have on the production of starch? Is any one color better than another? How could you test for starch production in other types of plants, such as grasses or ferns? Extract the green pigment from plants, and separate it using paper chromatography.

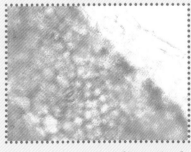 

Photomicrographs of bean leaf.

Seeds of Change

Legend has it that Johnny Appleseed was responsible for planting fruit trees throughout the United States. He may have been helped by the trees themselves. Seeds travel to new locations in lots of different ways. Some are eaten by birds and animals, which deposit them in new locations when they excrete them. Others attach themselves to pants legs and fur and hitch a ride. Certain seeds are shaped like tiny helicopter blades and are blown everywhere by the wind. Here's a science experiment to look at some ways in which this happens.

PURPOSE: To study how the shape of a seed affects how far it will travel.

HYPOTHESIS: Write a statement here to describe the effect of seed shape on the distance seeds travel. Your hypothesis should be specific to the experiment you choose to perform. Sample hypothesis: Seeds with a flat blade shape travel faster and farther than seeds that are round.

Materials

▶ different kinds of seeds with their attachments: pine cone seeds, maple tree seeds, milkweed seeds, etc.

▶ anemometer (if possible)

▶ hair dryer with at least 3 settings, or electric fan

▶ table

▶ large, empty room, such as a gymnasium or empty basement

▶ measuring tape

▶ broom

▶ adhesive tape

Some seeds.

Research Sources

▶ forest ranger

▶ professor of forestry

▶ botanist

▶ books or magazine articles on botany

▶ Related topics: aerodynamics, seed dispersal, germination, ovule, embryo, plant clustering, water, nutrients

Procedure

Record your data in your journal for each part of your experiment. Photograph or sketch your experiment.

1. Gather seeds with their attachments. Place each type in a bag and label the bags. Note: pine cone seeds are located within the individual cone sections.

2. If you have an anemometer, use it to measure the speed of the air blowing from the hair dryer as you work. Use a fan if you don't have a hair dryer. If you don't have an anemometer, record the hair dryer or fan settings and keep them the same for all the seeds.

3. Have a helper hold the hair dryer so that the nozzle is flat and parallel to the tabletop. Turn on the hair dryer to the lowest setting. Sprinkle about a teaspoon (5 mL) of seeds in front of the nozzle. Mark your starting place on the table with a bit of tape and use the measuring tape to measure how far each seed traveled and how far they spread. Try this with different kinds of seeds.

4. Repeat the experiment using a higher setting on the hair dryer.

Dandelion head at 60 ×.

Dandelion head at 60 ×.

Dandelion seed "parachute."

Breeze from hair dryer spins anemometer.

Results

What distances did the seeds travel? Was one type of seed a better traveler than the others? What happened to the seeds when you used the higher settings of the hair dryer? How much variation was there in distances traveled among seeds of the same type? Was there a relationship between the sizes of seeds of the same type and how far they traveled? What are the advantages to plants of seeds which do (or do not) travel away from the original plant?

Display Hints

Mount a hair dryer so that it can blow a large model of a seed that is attached to your display with strings or fishing line.

Display your seed samples: glue them to cards or onto the display board. Show drawings or photographs of the dispersal of the seeds. Use a bar graph to show the average distance traveled by each type of seed at each dryer or fan setting.

GOING FURTHER

Elementary Level

What conditions are necessary for seeds to germinate? Test to see if these are the same for several kinds of plants.

Junior High Level

Make some "seeds" out of various materials and test to see what shape of seed is the best for dispersal by water. Design a better seed dispersal system than is available in nature. What would it require? What is the best way to store seed so that it will later be able to germinate? Is this the same for all seeds? Design a seed package that will allow the seeds to stay fresh longer than the paper packages in which seeds usually are sold. Which types of seeds could you use it for? How would you modify it for different types of seeds?

Pine Cone Hygrometers

Is Mother Nature smarter than the weather forecaster on TV? Weather forecasters use satellite photos and sophisticated devices to describe the weather. One of the tools they use is a hygrometer, which measures the humidity of the air. You may have noticed that pine cones on damp days seem to be thinner than on dry days, and are closed up. If you take them inside and allow them to dry, they open and appear fatter.

PURPOSE: To use pine cones to measure the humidity of the air.

HYPOTHESIS: The seed cones close when exposed to higher humidity.

Materials

- mature pine cones from different kinds of conifers such as pine, fir, hemlock, and spruce trees*
- paper bags
- plastic bags
- ties for bags
- water
- barometer and hygrometer (optional)

Get several different sizes and several samples of each kind, at least 3 of each. Record in your journal which is which, by sketching, and label them.

Research Sources

- newspapers
- books on botany
- botanists
- plant field guides
- science or biology teachers
- books or magazine articles on conifers
- Related topics: barometric pressure, humidity, sensing cells, scales of a seed cone, seeds, moisture

Closed pine cones.

Open pine cones.

Procedure

For each part of the experiment, record the results in your journal and make sketches. Take photos if you can.

1. Take 3 specimens of seed cones from each kind of conifer. Divide the seed cones up into three groups.

2. Put one set of the seed cones in plastic bags with 1 tablespoon (5 mL) of water. Blow enough air into the bag to fill it and tie off the top. Leave them for about an hour. Watch what happens to the seed cones. Keep another set of the seed cones in the paper bag and place them in a dry place. Describe the appearance of these cones.

3. Place a set of seed cones outdoors in an area where they will be undisturbed and will not blow away. Watch the seed cones for several weeks and record whether the seed cones are opened or closed each day. Make note of the actual weather conditions each day, by listening to the radio or TV.

If you have a barometer or hygrometer, record the readings on these devices as well.

Results

What happened to the seed cones placed in the damp conditions of the plastic bag? What happened to the seed cones in the paper bag? What happened to the seed cones outdoors on dry days? What happened on wet days?

Display Hints

Display a closed seed cone and an open cone in glass jars or plastic bags. Mount a collection of different cones on your display board. Display weather reports from the newspaper for the dates on which you experimented.

GOING FURTHER

Elementary Level

Do different kinds of seed cones open and close to the same amount of moisture? Are some seed cones more responsive than others?

Junior High Level

Design and make a new type of hygrometer and compare it to the seed cone for accuracy in indicating the weather. See if cold affects the seed cones.

Some Like It Hot

You probably think that it takes longer for hot water to freeze than it does for cold water to freeze. There are two different phase changes involved. A phase change means going from one phase (solid, liquid, gas, or plasma) to another. Warm water will evaporate, or change from a liquid into a gas, faster than cold water will. Cold water will freeze, or change from a liquid into a solid, faster than warm water. With both of these things happening at the same time in open containers, you will sometimes get unexpected results!

PURPOSE: To see which freezes faster — hot water or cold water.

HYPOTHESIS: In an open container, hot water takes less time to freeze than cold water.

Materials

- ▶ several pairs of identical 8 oz (250 mL) containers, such as glass jars
- ▶ outdoor thermometer
- ▶ freezer
- ▶ kettle
- ▶ water
- ▶ measuring cup
- ▶ watch

Research Sources

▶ science teacher

▶ physics books or magazine articles on heat, freezing, phase changes, latent heat, heat transfer

Procedure

1. Fill one container with a cup (250 mL) of cold water. Measure and record the temperature of the water.

2. Fill a second container with one cup (250 mL) of hot water. Measure and record the temperature of the water.

3. Place both containers in the freezer of your refrigerator.

4. Without removing the containers from the freezer, measure the temperature of water in each container every 15 minutes.

Results

Which cools faster? How does the temperature change over time in each of the containers?

Display Hints

Display drawings or photographs of your setup. Draw a line graph to show the results over time for each container.

GOING FURTHER

Elementary Level

Try this experiment using different kinds of containers. Do you get the same results with metal containers as with glass containers? What about plastic containers? Do the size and shape of containers affect the results?

Junior High Level

Does circulation of air or water make any difference in your experiment? Test this by using a battery-operated fan in the freezer, or by stirring the water at regular intervals.

The Iceman Cometh

Have you ever skated on a frozen pond in the winter? Why can't you skate on the ocean? Does it ever get cold enough to freeze salt water? Why do they put salt on icy roads? For the answers to these and other questions, let's explore. Salt is used to lower the freezing temperature or freezing point of water when making ice cream. Salt is used to keep sidewalks and staircases free of ice in winter for the same reason.

PURPOSE: To see how impurities affect the freezing and melting points (temperatures) of water.

HYPOTHESIS: Water samples that contain more of an impurity such as salt or earth will take longer to freeze than pure water, and will freeze at a lower temperature than pure water samples.

Materials
▶ scientific or outdoor thermometer
▶ distilled water
▶ salt
▶ samples of water from different areas (lake, river, stream, ocean), tap water, bottled water

▶ pH test paper and chart*
▶ small glass canning jars or metal pie plates
▶ measuring cup

*pH is a measure of how acid or basic a solution is. The pH test paper changes color when it is inserted in a solution. The chart lets you "read" the color and know how acidic or basic the solution is. The smaller the pH, the more acidic the liquid is.

Different water samples.

Research Sources

▶ chemistry teachers

▶ books or magazine articles on the environment

▶ environmental groups

▶ city or government officials responsible for water quality

▶ Related topics: phase changes, solidification, melting point and freezing point, colligative properties, acid rain, water pollution

Procedure

1. Place 1 cup (250 mL) of each of the water samples in a glass jar and label each jar. Allow the samples to come to room temperature.

2. Measure the temperatures of the samples, and place them in a freezer, noting the time. Check the samples every 10 minutes until they are frozen. Note the time it took for each sample to freeze, and the freezing temperature.

3. Remove the samples from the freezer and watch as they begin to thaw. Note the condition of the samples and their temperatures every 5 minutes until the samples have completely thawed.

4. Take a 1 tablespoon (15 mL) sample of each jar and test the pH, following the package instructions on the pH paper.

5. Have an adult place the remainder of the samples in a

Setup showing thermometer and pH chart.

300°F (149°C) oven and heat them until all the water has evaporated. Describe what is left on the bottoms of the jars.

Results

Which samples took the longest to freeze or thaw? Which took the shortest time? How can you use your data to determine the melting and freezing points of the water samples? Is there a relationship between the pH of the water and its freezing and melting point? Do purer samples freeze and thaw at different temperatures than less pure samples?

Display Hints

Place the containers with the residue of the dried water samples on the display table. Display a bar graph showing the data from your different samples. Tape or glue your pH testing strips to a sheet of paper for display.

GOING FURTHER

Elementary Level

Add another substance to water, such as sand, sugar, or cream of tartar, to see how it affects the freezing point. Make ice cream using an old-fashioned ice cream maker. Why do you use ice and salt together to cool down the cream?

Junior High Level

Do a series of experiments to determine the relationship between the amount of salt in a water sample and its melting point.

Bubbleology

Bubbles are fun to blow, but is there any science involved in this activity? It turns out that the behavior of bubbles is very interesting science. Bubbles can be made from lots of different materials. Egg whites form bubbles when they are whipped. You may have discovered that milk will form bubbles when you blow air into it through a straw. Dishwashing liquid creates large, stable bubbles. Store-bought bubble solutions usually contain soap, water, and glycerin. Here is a way to create a science fair activity from an everyday substance.

PURPOSE: To see what bubble mixtures make the longest-lasting soap bubbles.

HYPOTHESIS: Write a statement here to describe how long you think the different types of bubbles last. Your hypothesis should be specific to the experiment you choose to perform. Sample hypothesis: Bubble solutions with glycerin make longer-lasting bubbles than solutions without glycerin. Solutions with a higher percentage of glycerin make longer-lasting bubbles than solutions with a lower percentage of glycerin.

Materials

- different brands of dishwashing liquid
- glycerine
- water
- various bubble blowers
- stopwatch
- containers
- cookie sheet
- video camera or still camera (if possible)

Research Sources

- reference books on the science of soap bubbles
- science museums
- Internet sites from science museums
- physics books
- chemistry books
- Related topics: thin-film behavior, surface tension, soaps

Bubbles in a jar.

Procedure

1. Prepare a standard soap bubble solution from each dishwashing liquid. Use ½ cup (125 mL) of dishwashing liquid for every 4 cups (1 liter) water. Add 1 tablespoon (5 mL) glycerine to the solution and mix.

2. Wet down a surface such as a cookie sheet with a thin layer of bubble solution. This is necessary because whenever a bubble touches a dry surface, it pops.

3. Change the amounts (proportions) of dishwashing liquid and glycerine in the best mixture and try the experiment again. Record the length of time it takes for a bubble to pop. Describe the bubbles you observe in each mixture. You may wish to videotape the bubbles or take pictures with a still camera.

Results

Which formula makes bubbles that last longest? Which mixture makes the biggest bubbles?

Display Hints

Blow bubbles in a jar, seal the jar, and record how long the bubbles last. Take photographs of the bubbles before they burst. Use colorful bubbles in designing the borders of your display sheets.

GOING FURTHER

Elementary Level

What is surface tension? Invent experiments to show what surface tension is. Measure the size of bubbles, using the outlines left on a tray or a piece of construction paper after they pop. Relate bubble size to the amount of time each takes to pop. Do small bubbles last longer?

Junior High Level

Experiment with different kinds and shapes of bubble blowers and bubble frames (for example, tetrahedron, square, octahedron, triangular prism, spiral). What factors can you discover that cause bubbles to join together to make larger bubbles? Develop a method for measuring the angles that bubbles make with each other. Experiment with bubbles of other substances besides soap. Do the angles vary in other substances? Which mixture makes the most colorful bubbles? Are the color changes in bubbles predictable? What color do the bubbles turn before they pop?

Bubble in cube.

Bubble in triangular solid.

Shake, Rattle, and Roll

You probably have seen television reports or newspaper articles about the damage from major earthquakes. Did you notice that some buildings collapse during an earthquake, while others seem undamaged? In high-risk areas, building are supposed to be designed to with-stand moderate to severe earthquakes and are built with materials which will allow the structures to sway, instead of collapsing. What features of building design help prevent destruction in quake-prone areas?

PURPOSE: To design and test the performance of several different building shapes in a simulated earthquake.

HYPOTHESIS: Write a statement here to describe the effect of an earthquake on various building designs. Sample hypothesis: Short, broad structures are more stable when shaken in soft sand than tall, thin ones.

Materials

- ▶ large cardboard box or plastic tote container with handles
- ▶ dry clean sand to fill the container to a depth of 4 inches (10 cm)
- ▶ plastic interlocking blocks like Lego™ or Duplo™
- ▶ washing machine
- ▶ watch with second hand or stopwatch
- ▶ camera (if possible)

Research Sources

▶ government pamphlets on earthquakes

▶ architects, municipal planners

▶ engineers

▶ books or articles in magazines on building design, liquefaction, pressure, building structures, engineering

Procedure

1. Fill the cardboard box or tote container with sand. Make sure the container is large enough to contain your building

designs, but small enough for you to shake it.

2. Use the interlocking blocks to make a 4 inch (10 cm) cube. Place the cube in the box of sand.

3. Place the box on top of a washing machine. Turn the machine to the spin cycle and observe and note the positions of the blocks over 5 minutes. If you wish, you can take photos of this to use in your display.

4. Add foundations of different shapes onto the bottom of the cube. You may wish to try a thick central pillar, or several thin posts, or even an open box shape. Be creative; try several different designs. Each time, place the cube with its new foundation in the sandbox and place the box on the washing machine while it is on the spin cycle. Note how the foundation affects the movement of the cube on the sand.

Results

How long did each building stay on top of the sand? What amount of shifting occurred for each? Which design appeared to be the most stable? Which was the least stable?

Display Hints

Place some of your foundation designs on the display table. Include photographs or drawings of the designs after they have moved and settled in the sand.

GOING FURTHER

Elementary Level

Repeat the experiment with a structure based on triangles, such as a geodesic dome. Repeat the experiment, but vary the kind of materials in your container. Try gravel or earth. If you live in an area that is prone to earthquakes, design a survey to determine what kinds of planning families in your area have done to prepare for earthquakes and to prevent damage to their houses. Compare their responses to the suggestions given for your area.

Junior High Level

Design a shaker which will allow you to increase or decrease the amount of shaking in the box by a measured amount. Use other materials to make more realistic models of the other parts of buildings in addition to the foundations.

Bull's-Eye

Have you ever felt a small tremor or movement of the earth, or an earthquake? If so, you probably felt the movement, but you couldn't tell where the actual earthquake started. Earthquakes are caused by movement of the large plates of rock and earth that make up the Earth's crust. Scientists all over the world are monitoring earthquake activities, to try to learn more about them and predict their occurrence. For each quake, they measure the tremors to locate the epicenter, the place on the surface of the Earth directly above the focus where the earthquake began.

One device used to measure earthquakes is a seismograph, which measures and records the amount of ground motion during an earthquake. At least 3 seismographic stations are required to locate the epicenter of an earthquake. Let's see how you can use a homemade seismograph to tell where the shaking action is coming from.

PURPOSE: To try to determine the epicenter of a simulated earthquake.

HYPOTHESIS: Seismograph tracings are smaller when they are made from a location further away from the epicenter of a quake than they are when the epicenter is nearby.

Materials
▶ cube-shaped cardboard box about 12 to 16 inches (30 to 40 cm) on a side
▶ craft knife
▶ ruler
▶ roll of adding machine paper tape
▶ 8 ounce (250 mL) flexible plastic container (like the type used for yogurt)
▶ hammer and nail
▶ tape
▶ felt-tipped pen
▶ string
▶ small pebbles, marbles, or gravel
▶ pencil

Research Sources
▶ geologists
▶ government pamphlets on earthquakes
▶ front section of telephone books from earthquake-prone areas (check your library for these)

- ▶ disaster planning or emergency services
- ▶ general science books
- ▶ Related topics: inertia, types of earthquake waves, magnitude, triangulation, seismographs and seismograms, speed of earthquake waves, lateral and vertical motion

Procedure
(see construction diagrams)

1. Have an adult use a craft knife to remove the lid flaps from the box. Lay the box on its side. Have the adult cut a 1 inch (2.5 cm) diameter circle out of the center of the side of the box that is now at the top.

2. Then have the adult cut two narrow slits for the adding machine paper to slide through. The first should be in the middle of the back fold on what is now the bottom of the box. The second slit should be centered left to right on the side of the box that is now at the bottom; the slit should be about 2 inches (5 cm) in from the box opening.

3. With the roll of paper in back, outside the box, slide the adding machine tape from outside the box into the box through the first slit and out through the second slit so that it moves freely along the bottom surface. Set the box aside.

4. Have an adult use a hammer and nail to make two holes across the container's rim from each other and about ¼ inch (0.5 cm) down from the rim of the plastic container. Use the nail or a craft knife to

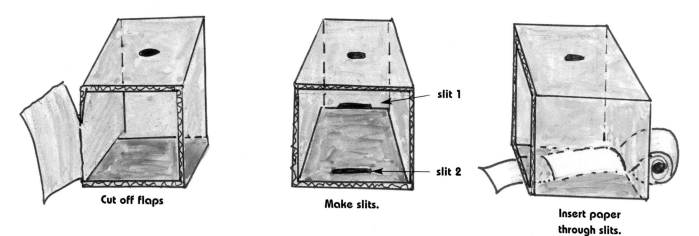

Cut off flaps

Make slits.

slit 1

slit 2

Insert paper through slits.

Preparing the box for the seismograph.

Make holes in container.

Insert pen.

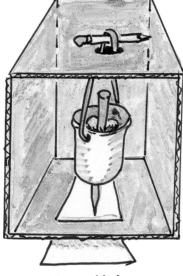

All assembled.

make a hole in the center of the bottom of the container just large enough to hold the felt-tipped pen. Place the pen upright in the hole so that the felt tip sticks out of the bottom about 1 inch (2.5 cm). Thread a piece of string through the holes near the rim of the cup to make a loop. Tie the ends inside. Fill the cup with pebbles, marbles, or gravel so that the pen is firmly held in place.

5. Tape a pencil in place across the hole in the top of the box. Pull the string loop up through the hole and over the pencil. Adjust the ends of the string holding the plastic container so that the felt-tipped pen can just touch the adding machine paper. Gently pull on the end of the paper to check if the

pen can make a line. If not, adjust the height of the pen. Have a helper tap the table lightly while you pull on the adding machine paper to see how the device works. This is your seismograph.

6. Place the seismograph on the floor in one corner of a large, empty room with a wooden floor, like a school gym or a dance studio.

The completed seismograph.

Rooms with concrete or tile floors should not be used. Have an adult helper jump up and down several times at a distance of 2 feet (60 cm) from the seismograph. Pull gently on the end of

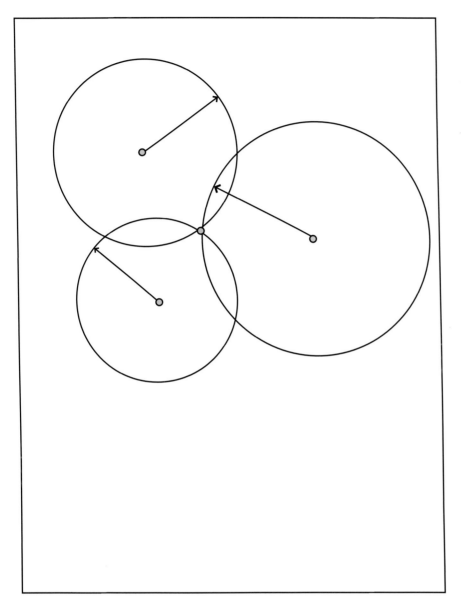

The place where the three circles based on the seismograph tracings intersect is the epicenter of the "quake" (orange dot). The places where the seismographs were recorded are marked with blue dots.

the paper to make a tracing of the pen motion while the person jumps. When the person jumps, the floor probably will move (vibrate). But the hanging pen with its cup of pebbles tends to stay in place because of inertia. Measure the width of the pen tracing from peak to peak, using a ruler to see how far across the strip the pen swings for each vibration. Count how many vibration lines were made when the person jumped. Repeat this with the seismograph at distances of 4, 6, 8, and 10 feet (1.2 m, 1.8 m, 2.4 m, 3.0 m) from the jumper. Label your seismographic tape to show which markings are for each distance.

7. Draw a scale diagram of the room, with the location of the seismograph shown. Have an adult helper jump up and down several times in one location. Move the seismograph to each of the four corners of the room, and repeat this, with the jumping adult remaining in the same location.

8. Compare your pen tracings to the ones obtained in step 6 to determine the approximate distance of the jumping adult from the seismograph in each corner. The same size jump should result in the same size tracing, if made at the same distance. Draw circles on your diagram to scale. Each circle should have the seismograph at the center and have as its radius the distance from the seismograph to the person jumping.

Results

What happens to the seismograph tracing when someone jumps near the device? What is the relationship between the distance from the seismograph and the size of the tracing? Where do the circles on your diagram overlap?

Display Hints

Draw a line graph showing the average width of the pen strokes, related to the distance the seismograph was from the jumping adult when the pen strokes were made. Display several of your maps with the circles shown. Place your seismograph on the display table with a fresh pen and lots of adding machine paper so you can demonstrate how it works.

GOING FURTHER

Elementary Level

Look at actual seismograms (drawings made by seismographs). You may find some on the Internet. How are they different from the ones you made? How could you change your seismograph to make your seismograms more like real ones? Design a winding device to make it easier to move the paper through your seismograph.

Junior High Level

The design we used is for a seismograph that measures the horizontal (side-to-side) component of earthquake waves. Design a seismograph that allows you to measure the vertical (up-down) component.

Tracing the Stars

Over 3000 years ago, Chinese astronomers used a device that looked like a flat jade bracelet with irregular notches in it to study the stars. When this tool was held at arm's length, with the Pole Star in the center, the other stars matched the notches in the outer circle. There were different patterns for each season. This was one of the earliest star charts. A star chart is a sky map that helps you find the constellations by matching clusters of stars on the chart to those you find in the sky. A constellation is a group of stars that seemed to early astronomers to form a picture in the sky; for example, an animal or god. Here is an easy way to create your own personal star chart.

PURPOSE: To make a star chart to examine stellar and planetary motion.

HYPOTHESIS: The stars move across the night sky from east to west. Some objects in the sky move faster than others.

Materials
▶ 40 inches (102 cm) of stiff wire
▶ clear cellophane wrap
▶ clear cellophane tape
▶ bottle of white correction fluid
▶ small label
▶ pen or pencil
▶ black piece of construction paper
▶ star chart for the location, times, and dates at which the observations are made
▶ labels

Research Sources
▶ astronomers
▶ planetariums
▶ books and magazines on astronomy, planetary motion, parallax
▶ science teachers
▶ Internet sites or software packages on astronomy

Procedure

1. You will need a helper. Fold the wire so that it forms a square 10 inches × 10 inches (25 cm × 25 cm). Tape the wire ends together.
2. Cover the square with clear cellophane wrap and tape the cellophane to the wire frame.
3. On a clear night, go outside and hold your frame up to a section of the sky where the stars are shining brightly.
4. Hold the frame at arm's length and observe the stars through the frame.
5. While you hold the frame as still as possible, have your helper use the correction fluid to place a small mark on the cellophane on the place where you see each bright star, planet, or the moon. You and your helper can take turns doing this, but don't change the position of the frame. You may want to paint or tape a line on the ground to mark where you stand.

6. When you have finished your chart, go indoors. Place the frame you created over a black piece of paper.
7. Compare your chart to a star chart to identify which constellations you mapped.
8. Place a small label on your homemade star chart, noting the date and time you created your chart, and the names of the constellations.
9. Make another frame and chart for the same section of the night sky at different times, over several evenings. Compare the positions of the constellations.

Results

Which constellations were you able to identify? How did the stars or planets you identified move across the night sky? What is the difference between the motion of nearby objects like the moon and planets and the motion of the stars, which are further away?

Display Hints

Mount your star charts on black paper and display them. Show the sections of a commercial star chart to which they correspond.

GOING FURTHER

Elementary Level

Choose one constellation and observe how it moves from one night to the next. Use a tree or lamppost as a reference. A long time ago, people invented drawings of animals, gods, or other subjects to help them remember the positions of the stars. Make up your own shapes out of the stars you observed to help you remember them.

Junior High Level

Chart the motion of a constellation through an entire night; get an adult to help you. Research light pollution. Travel to a location where you can observe the stars with fewer lights, if possible. Where are the best locations for telescopes nowadays? Build a reflecting telescope. Use it to make more detailed observations of the things you can see in the night sky.

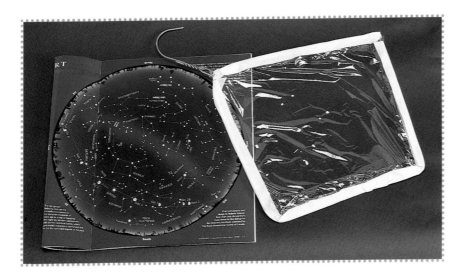

Oil Slick

Are you allowed to use the sprinkler on your lawn in the summertime? In many areas the supply of fresh water in the summer is so low that there are restrictions on when or even if you can use sprinklers. With global warming, cities around the world are suffering from water shortages. Many cities are studying ways in which they can limit consumption of water and also conserve the amount in their watershed. During hot weather, water use is high, and there is evaporation of water from the reservoirs. How can this evaporation be reduced? A covering layer that prevents evaporation is one way. The challenge is to find a material that is safe to drink and safe for any local wildlife. Oil is not the best choice for this, but it does illustrate the principle.

PURPOSE: To see if a layer of oil can prevent or reduce evaporation of water.

HYPOTHESIS: Adding oil to the top of the water sample slows evaporation. Increasing amounts of oil decreases the rate of evaporation.

Materials

▶ measuring cup
▶ water
▶ 5 small wide-mouth glass canning jars
▶ cooking oil
▶ eyedropper
▶ measuring spoons
▶ ruler
▶ labels

Research Sources

▶ chemistry teachers
▶ books on the environment, evaporation, phase changes, vapor pressure, water quality, oils, respiration
▶ magazine articles on water supply and demand
▶ environmental groups
▶ city or government officials responsible for water quality

Procedure

1. Use a measuring cup to half-fill each of the 5 jars with exactly the same volume of water. Put a label on each jar.
2. Leave the first jar with no oil. Add a drop of cooking oil to the second jar. Add 5 drops of cooking oil to the third jar. Add a teaspoon (5 mL) of cooking oil to the fourth jar. Add a tablespoon (15 mL) of cooking oil the fifth jar.
3. Place the jars, uncovered, in a warm spot where they can be undisturbed for several days. Make sure that they will all

receive the same amount of sunlight.

4. Measure the height of water in the jars each day for two weeks. Record your results.

Results

Which of the jars had the lowest level of water (evaporated the most); which had the highest (evaporated the least)?

Display Hints

Make a line graph with a line for each jar drawn in a different color, showing the results for each day.

GOING FURTHER

Elementary Level

Do an experiment to study the effect of temperature on evaporation. What is the effect of using larger or smaller jars? What happens if you cover jars containing water with plastic wrap instead of adding oil?

Junior High Level

Repeat the experiment with other liquid materials instead of oil. Devise other ways to reduce evaporation. Test to see if freshwater evaporates faster than salt water.

Down the Drain

There was a time when toilet paper came in bright colors and was printed with designs. This kind of toilet paper is far less common now, because the dyes were harmful to the environment. Recycled and unbleached toilet papers are now commonly available and have a much lower impact on the environment. Your parents may have told you that toilet paper is the only paper which should be flushed in your toilet. But are your parents right? Let's look to see what happens to the paper.

PURPOSE: To determine which papers break down the fastest in the sewage system.

HYPOTHESIS: Write a statement here to describe the way in which different papers break down in water. Your hypothesis should be specific to the experiment you choose to perform. Sample hypothesis: Toilet paper breaks down the fastest of all papers in water and does not need to be treated with any additives to assist in its breakdown.

Materials

▶ kitchen scale
▶ scissors
▶ several different paper samples (toilet papers of more than one brand, tissues, paper towels, wet wipes, facial tissues, paper napkins)
▶ quart (1 L) glass jars (the same number as your paper samples) with lids
▶ masking tape or labels
▶ measuring cup
▶ water
▶ thermometer
▶ watch
▶ camera
▶ vinegar
▶ large (gallon or more) container for water
▶ household bleach (to be used with adult supervision only)
▶ salt
▶ camera, if possible

Research Sources

▶ sewage treatment facilities

▶ magazine articles on sewage treatment

▶ government agencies

▶ environmental groups

▶ Related topics: environment, environmental science, fibers, pulp and paper treatment

Procedure

1. Weigh each paper sample on the scale and be sure that they all have the same weight. If necessary, trim the samples to the correct weight.
2. Place each sample in a separate glass jar and label the jars to indicate what is in them.
3. Fill a gallon container with tap water and let it come to room temperature.
4. Measure exactly 2 cups (500 mL) of room-temperature water into the first jar, making

sure to note the temperature.
5. Shake the jar for one minute. Then take a photo of it and make and record your observations. Do this four more times on the same sample, for a total of 5 minutes of shaking. Put the jar aside and note the time.
6. Repeat steps 4 and 5 for each of the paper samples. Place the jars in a warm, sunny place and check them once a day for several days. Note any changes.
7. Repeat steps 4 to 6 using vinegar, bleach, or salt water on a kind of paper that doesn't break down much in water alone, such as facial tissue.

Results

Which paper broke down the fastest? Which took the longest? Did any of the papers not break down at all? How did using the vinegar, bleach, and salt water affect the amount of time the paper took to break down?

Photomicrograph of edge of torn paper.

Display Hints

Set up a microscope with fiber samples. Display samples of the original paper. Make a table listing the samples, with observations at 1, 2, 3, 4, and 5 minutes. Your observations could be in words, or could include photographs of the samples. Create a bar graph comparing the breakdown times of the samples.

GOING FURTHER

Elementary Level

Look at the fibers from the different types of paper using a microscope. How might the length and size of the fibers affect their ability to break down? Test your hypothesis.

Junior High Level

Analyze the current method of sewage treatment in your community and devise an alternative method. Create an experiment to evaluate the use of bleach used in treating paper or sewage. What are the benefits? What are the concerns? Learn about the components of paper and create a more environmentally friendly paper product.

Something Old, Something New

Recycling paper is good for the environment. Using recycled paper means fewer trees need to be cut down to make paper. Less room is taken up in landfills with paper if it is recycled. One problem with recycling paper is that the more times paper is recycled, the weaker the paper becomes. Here's a way to measure the strength of recycled paper compared to unrecycled paper.

PURPOSE: To compare the strengths of recycled and new paper.

HYPOTHESIS: New paper is stronger than recycled paper.

Materials

- sheets of medium-weight bond paper, white or colored
- water
- measuring cup
- electric blender
- large, deep, rectangular disposable foil roasting pan
- wire coat hanger
- nylon stocking or one leg cut off pantyhose
- elastic band
- newspaper, blotting paper, or felt
- scissors
- ruler
- heavy lead fishing sinker

Research Sources

- books on papermaking
- pulp and paper technicians
- Related topics: environmental science, fibers, tensile strength

Procedure

1. Tear two sheets of the bond paper into pieces about ½ inch (1 cm) square. Place the pieces in the blender and add water to half-fill the blender. If you are in an elementary grade, do the next part with an adult helper. Use the blender on "pulse" several times until the mixture looks like runny oatmeal. This should take about one minute. If the paper gets caught up in the blender blades, add more water and shake the blender container to loosen the paper. Warning: If the blades aren't turning and the paper is caught, turn off the blender, as you can damage the motor. Remove the container from the blender and unstick the blades.

2. Pour the paper-and-water mixture into the roasting pan.

Repeat Step 1 until the roasting pan is about half full. Record the number of sheets of paper you used and their size. The mixture should be thin and soupy. If it is as thick as porridge, add a little extra water.

3. Hold the metal hanger by the hook and pull down on the bottom of the hanger to stretch it lengthwise. Slip the bottom of the hanger into the foot of the nylon stocking and stretch the nylon gently. Secure the nylon to the twisted part of the hanger with an elastic band.

4. Grasp the sides of the hanger through the nylon and stretch the hanger to make a large square shape. This is your screen. The screen should be

Sample papers

small enough to fit inside the roasting pan, but large enough to make a piece of paper about 8 inches (20 cm) square.

5. Stir the paper-and-water mixture with your hand. Immediately slide the screen down the side and along the bottom of the container, making sure that the mixture covers all of the screen.

6. Carefully lift the screen up through the mixture, allowing the water to pass through the stocking. Don't touch the top of the screen containing the pulp mixture. When the water stops dripping, transfer the screen, pulp-side up, to a layer of newspaper. Place several sheets of newspaper on top of the pulp and turn the whole thing over. Peel off the layer of newspaper and the screen. Repeat steps 5 and 6 until there is not enough pulp left to make any more sheets of paper. Note the number of sheets of paper you produced.

Paper being made.

Let the recycled paper dry overnight.

7. Test the strength of the paper. Cut several ½ inch × 8 inch (1 × 20 cm) strips of the original paper. Tie a heavy lead fishing weight (sinker) to the middle of a 15-inch (37 cm) piece of string. Tie the ends of the string to either end of a pencil.

8. Have a helper hold the strip of original paper by the ends and stretch it gently. Hang the weight below the paper with the pencil 6 inches (15 cm) over the top (see photo). Make sure that if the weight drops, it will not damage anything.

9. Drop the pencil onto the strip of paper. If the strip tears, repeat the test with two strips, one on top of the other. See how many strips of paper it takes to hold the dropped weight. Note your findings.

10. Repeat steps 7 through 9 with the recycled paper.

Results

How many pieces of original paper did you use and how many pieces of recycled paper did you get? How many pieces of each type of paper did it take to support the dropped weight?

Display Hints

Display samples of the different types of paper made and used. Display your testing apparatus with strips for people to test.

Paper being tested.

GOING FURTHER

Elementary Level

How many times can paper be recycled and still be usable? Will paper strips break more easily if they are cut lengthwise or widthwise on the paper? Does it matter which way the paper fibers are aligned? Find out how watermarks are made and try designing a device to make watermarks on your paper.

Junior High Level

Research the different techniques used in the paper-making industry to test paper. Design a device to do one or more of these tests on your paper samples. What are the effects of changes in water content and temperature on the strength of paper?

What Counts?

There are many science fair projects you can do by comparing different brands and prices of a product to see which is the best value. Some things you might want to use are: popcorn, chocolate chip cookies, canned or dehydrated chicken soup, hot dogs (frankfurters), batteries, oranges, and orange juice.

PURPOSE: To study the relationship between price and quality in household items.
HYPOTHESIS: Write a statement that relates the product you test to its cost. For example: The most expensive popcorn produces the fewest unpopped kernels.

Materials
▶ several brands of the same product (for example, popcorn, chocolate chip cookies, soups, hot dogs, batteries, oranges, orange juice)
▶ camera (if possible)

Research Sources
▶ consumer books, magazines, Internet sites
▶ advertisements in magazines
▶ commercials on television
▶ Related topics: measurement, value, cost analysis

Procedure
Follow the procedure for the products you are testing:
1. Popcorn: Which brand gives you the most popcorn and the fewest unpopped kernels?

Compare the price to the volume of popped popcorn you get. Make sure to measure the raw popcorn and pop all the brands using the same method.

2. Chocolate chip cookies: Which brand gives you the most chocolate

chips per cookie or per box? Compare the number of chocolate chips to the price of the box. One way to measure the number of chocolate chips per cookie or per box is to soak the cookies in cold water, and then strain the mixture using a sieve.

3. Soup: Which chicken noodle soup gives you the most chicken per can? Separate the noodles, chicken, and vegetables and compare the brands and the prices.

4. Hot dogs: Which hot dog has the most meat, the least fat, the least filler, the least water? Dry out samples in an oven to get their weight without water. Read the product labels to compare the contents.

5. Batteries: Which battery lasts the longest? For each brand, use the same size battery in a toy or piece of equipment and record how long each battery lasts. Use rechargeable and disposable batteries.

6. Orange juice: Which juice tastes most like freshly squeezed oranges? Pour several different brands of orange juice in small servings. Label the cups 1, 2, 3, 4, etc. Have volunteers taste a glass of fresh-squeezed orange juice; then blindfold the volunteers and have them taste several different brands.

Include a sample of freshly squeezed orange juice among your test samples and see if people can tell the difference.

7. Oranges: Compare the amount of juice you get from different types of oranges. Which orange gives you the most juice? Which has the most pits? Compare the amount of juice to the cost of the fruit.

Results

The results will vary depending on which products you test. Your results should include a discussion of the questions posed in whichever of the procedures you used in the project.

Display Hints

Display photos taken during the experiment. Bring the cans or containers from the various items. You can mount labels directly on your display board. Word of warning: It is not a wonderful idea to bring foods into the science fair. Your display will be swamped by hungry scientists, anxious to test your experiment.

GOING FURTHER

Elementary Level

Choose a product you use every day, or one you have seen advertised. Test to see if it really does what the advertising claims. Do a survey of people who use the product to see if they think so. Compare the store brands or generic brands with the nationally advertised brands of products. Which is the better value?

Junior High Level

Sometimes the manufacturer of a product uses scientific tests to make claims about the product (for example, measuring the acidity of a soap). Repeat these tests, using the product and a competitor's product, and compare the results.

Bed of Nails

You may have seen pictures or a demonstration of a person lying on a bed of nails. Have you ever wondered why the nails don't poke through the person? We sure did, especially when a melon dropped onto the bed of nails broke apart and splattered. As you can see in the photograph (page 85), we tried this ... and lived to tell the tale. The trick is to lie down very slowly so that every part of your body touches the nails at the same time and to stand up the same way. This keeps the weight on each individual nail equal, so that the pressure each nail point exerts on your body is not too high. It takes an expert to do this safely, as well as a helper to aid the person in getting up and down. We advise you not to try this at home; however, here's a safe way to try a pressure experiment without causing you pain.

PURPOSE: To see how increasing the number of nails affects the amount of pressure on each individual nail, using a balloon.

HYPOTHESIS: A balloon will pop if placed on a single nail point, but will not pop if it is placed on several nail points.

Materials
▶ 1 gallon (4 L) plastic bucket
▶ balloons
▶ 2 dozen 1-inch (2.5 cm) nails
▶ hammer
▶ book
▶ video camera or still camera
▶ water (optional)

Research Sources
▶ science museums
▶ physics teachers
▶ books about science magic
▶ physics books
▶ Related topics: pressure, surface area, weight, mass, density

Procedure
1. Hammer a nail into the middle of the bottom of the plastic bucket from the outside in, so that the head of the nail is on the outside and the point is sticking up inside the bucket bottom.

record your findings in your journal.

3. Hammer 2 nails, several inches apart, into the bucket.

4. Repeat Step 2. Are the results different than before?

5. Try the experiment several times, each time using additional nails, until you have used all 24 nails.

Results

How many nails were necessary before the balloon stopped bursting? Did it matter how the nails were spaced?

Display Hints

Use a Pinpoint® toy or another kind of pin toy to show the different surface area when you push up one pin, compared to pushing up several pins. Display your bucket with nails, and use balloons to show the

2. Inflate a balloon so that it will fit loosely in the bucket. Slowly place the balloon inside the bucket, so that the rounded end of the balloon touches the nail point. Videotape, photograph, or sketch this step, and

technique to the judges. Tie or tape inflated balloons (even helium balloons) to your display board. Use a balloon design border on your display board.

Shapes made with Pinpoint® movable pin toy.

Bed of nails at Science World, Vancouver, B.C., Canada.

Author Leslie Johnstone tests the bed of nails.

GOING FURTHER

Elementary Level

Measure the length and width of your feet in inches or centimeters. Multiply the length and width together; then multiply the total by two to get the approximate surface area of your feet. Weigh yourself, and divide your weight by the area of your feet. Compare the number you get for your body to the number your parent or teacher gets for the same calculation. Does this explain why some adults complain that their feet hurt at the end of the day? Try the same calculation using the bottom walking surface of a pair of high heels instead of feet. Would you expect feet to be more comfort-

able in high heels or in flat shoes? Ask someone who wears high heels how she feels.

Junior High Level

Add another step to the experiment. When you have enough nails so that the balloon doesn't burst, try adding weights to the top of the balloon. Does the balloon stay inflated? Vary the weight of the objects on top. How much can the balloon hold before it breaks? Does it matter whether you place the weight or drop it? Does the type of balloon make a difference? Will a thicker balloon keep from popping longer? Is the amount of inflation important? Does it matter if you fill the balloon with water?

Will It Fly?

There's nothing more fun than taking a kite out to an open field on a windy day. It's great to send a kite flying high into the sky. Have you ever noticed how some kites are easy to launch while others take a lot of effort? Why do you think this is? Why do some kites have tails? Alexander Graham Bell, the inventor of the telephone, and his wife Mabel studied kites to help them design early aircraft. Studying kites is an interesting introduction to the science of aerodynamics.

PURPOSE: To explore the best shape for a kite and the effect of adding a tail to the kite.

HYPOTHESIS: A kite with a tail remains in the air longer than the same kite without a tail.

Materials
▶ several kites, all about the same size, of different kinds (triangular, box) and materials (plastic, parachute material, Mylar™, polystyrene)
▶ different lengths of kite tail material
▶ kite string
▶ tape measure
▶ watch
▶ still camera or video camera (if possible)

Research Sources
▶ books on kites and flight
▶ airplane designers or manufacturers
▶ parachuting instructors
▶ Related topics: air pressure and stability, bridling techniques, lift and drag, airfoils, kite design

Note: Do not fly kites near high-tension electric wires, near trees, or during a thunderstorm.

Procedure

1. Assemble several kites and photograph them or draw them in your journal. Note the manner in which the string attaches to the kites.

2. Go outside on a windy day. Have a helper stand about 25 feet (8 meters) away from you, holding the kite. Have the helper release the kite while you hold the string. Does the kite rise into the air? Repeat the same technique with all the kites.

3. Attach a tail to one of the kites. Does this make the kite easier to fly? Try kite tails of different lengths.

Results

Which kites are the easiest to launch? Which are the hardest? Which rise the highest? How does increasing the length of the tail affect the kite?

Display Hints

Mount kites over the display, especially smaller models. Make a "wind tunnel" with a hair dryer and small versions of the kite for demonstration. A kite motif on the borders of the pages can make a colorful addition to your display.

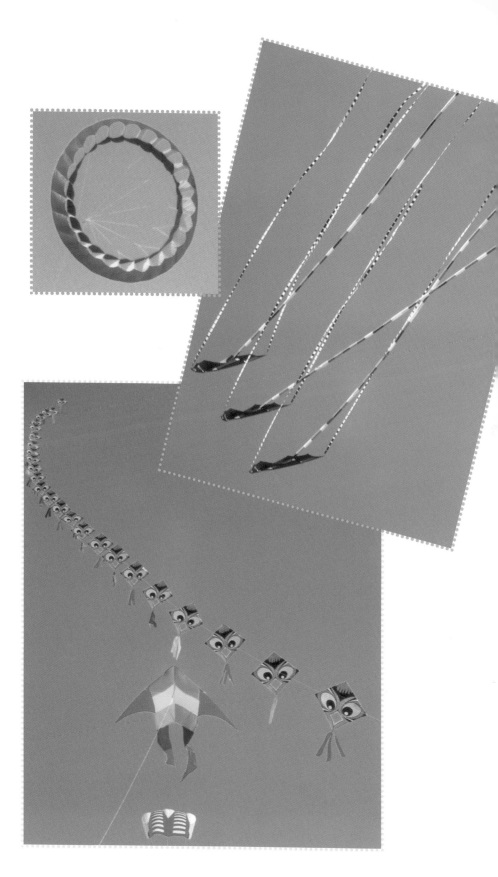

Elementary Level

Is a bigger kite easier to launch than a smaller kite? Experiment to see which material makes a kite that is:

- ▶ the easiest to launch;
- ▶ the easiest to keep aloft;
- ▶ the easiest to maneuver. Experiment with designs in the same way.

Junior High Level

Test to see whether kites made of parachute material (or thin, ripstop nylon) and designed like a parachute are easier to launch than flat kites. How does a "Hawaiian kite" fly? Experiment to see how the string placement affects the stability of the kite. Which kinds of kites fly best in a strong wind? Are they the same ones that fly best in a light wind? Do some tests to see if humidity affects how a kite flies.

Weigh to Go

The mass of an object is the same wherever you measure it. Mass is measured using a balance, which compares the mass to a standard mass. Weight depends on the outside forces acting on an object. You can lose weight by traveling to the moon, where gravity is less, but you couldn't lose mass. Mass is measured by scientists in grams or pounds, and weight is measured in newtons, but most people give the weight of objects using the mass units instead of the actual weight units.

When you are swimming and you lift a heavy weight under water, it seems easy to move. When you take the object out of the water, it seems to get heavier. What happens to change the weight of the object?

PURPOSE: To examine the difference in the weight of an object in and out of water.

HYPOTHESIS: When objects are placed in water, their weight is less than in air.

Materials

▶ fish-weighing scale or spring scale

▶ several solid objects of various weights; for example, a rock, a full can or jar, a screwdriver

▶ string

▶ large wide-mouthed glass jar, big enough to hold your objects

▶ measuring cup

▶ bottle of nail polish

Research Sources

▶ physics books

▶ science teachers

▶ magazines or articles on ship and boat design

▶ Related topics: water pressure, weight, buoyancy, displacement

Procedure

1. Using your measuring cup, fill the container 50 mL at a time and mark the milliliters on the outside with the nail polish. Then pour off some of the water. Draw a line on the outside of the container to show the final water level.

2. Tie a string around an object, and attach the other end of the string to a fish scale. Weigh the object with the fish scale, and record the weight in your journal.

3. Using the fish scale, slowly lower an object into the water so that it is completely submerged. Record the weight of the object when it is in the water. What is the difference, if any, between the object's weight in and out of the water?

4. Have a helper draw a line on the outside of the container to show the water level while the object is submerged in the container.

5. Repeat steps 1 to 4 with other projects.

Weighing the object.

Results

What did the objects weigh in and out of water? How much did the water rise when the object was placed inside? Did the weights of objects that were the same size and made of similar materials change by the same amount when they were placed in water?

Display Hints

You usually aren't allowed to have liquids in your display, so you probably can't display the actual setup of the experiment. Instead use photographs of items in and out of water, attached to a fish scale. Use a bar graph to show the weights in and out of water, and the volume change (or height of the water) for each object tested.

GOING FURTHER

Elementary Level

Try the experiment in salt water. Is there a difference in weight in and out of salt and fresh water? Does the amount of salt in the water affect your results?

Junior High Level

While the object is submerged, have a helper remove water until the original water level is reached. Weigh the water you have removed by placing it in a plastic bag and tying the bag to the scale. Is it equal to the weight of the object?

Magnetic Erasers

Many products have warning labels, cautioning the user not to place the item near a magnet. Have you ever wondered why? It turns out that the information on videotapes or audiotapes is made by arranging magnetic material in a specific pattern. When a strong magnet is brought close to these materials, it scrambles the coded messages, and they no longer make sense. Instead of beautiful music or a computer program, you are left with useless information. Which types of devices are affected by magnets? Let's find out.

PURPOSE: To study the effect of magnets on recorded items.
HYPOTHESIS: Magnets damage video and audiotapes but not compact discs (CDs).

Materials
▶ strong magnet or electromagnet
▶ weaker magnet or an iron nail magnetized by the stronger magnet
▶ music compact disc (CD)*
▶ videotape*
▶ audiotape*

▶ CD player
▶ tape recorder
▶ videocassette recorder

Research Sources
▶ science teachers
▶ physics teachers
▶ books on how things work
▶ Related subjects: magnetism, information storage and retrieval

*These should be ones that you don't want to use again.

Procedure
1. Record in your journal what information is stored on each of the items you are testing. Play a little of each to see how clear the information is on each format.
2. Hold a weak magnet near each of the objects. Play them again. Is there any change in the stored information?
3. Hold a strong magnet, such as an electromagnet, near each of the objects.
4. Play the tape or CD again, and listen to it. Did the

stronger magnet have any effect on the information?

Results

What changes did you observe in each item after placing it near the weak and strong magnets?

Display Hints

Display a portable CD player with the CD you used. Display a portable tape recorder with the tape used. Show the different magnets you used.

GOING FURTHER

Elementary Level

Make an electromagnet. Experiment with ways to make the electromagnet stronger.

Junior High Level

How strong does a magnet have to be before it affects information on an item? What materials can you use to shield the items from the magnetism? What is the effect of increased distance? How far away do magnets have to be from the tape before the magnets have no effect? Does temperature have any effect on magnetic action? Design a device which will code magnetic messages onto tape.

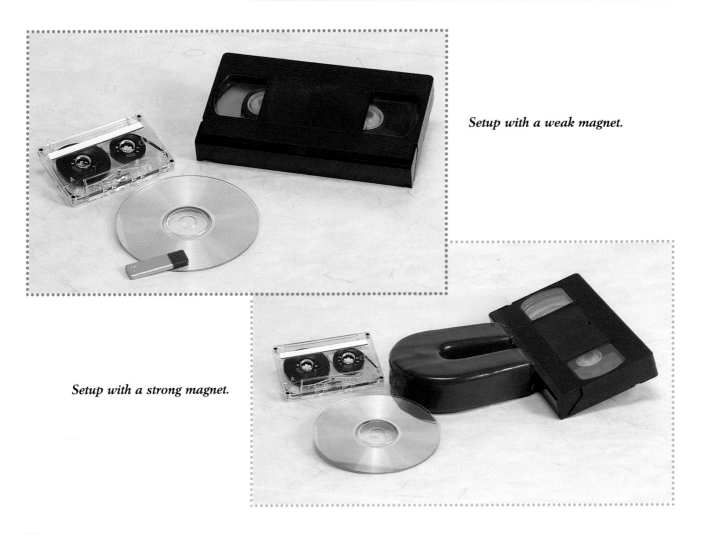

Setup with a weak magnet.

Setup with a strong magnet.

Streamlined

When you water your garden or wash the family car using a hose, have you ever noticed how the angle at which you hold the hose affects how far the stream of water goes? Where is the best place to stand, and how should you hold the hose to get the stream of water to travel the farthest? If you keep the water pressure the same, is it better to point the hose straight ahead, or does the water travel farther when it makes an arc?

PURPOSE: To determine which angle of a hose allows water to go the farthest.

HYPOTHESIS: Write a statement here to describe the effect of the angle and water force on the distance water will travel after leaving a hose. Your hypothesis should be specific to the experiment you perform. Sample hypothesis: When the hose is placed at an angle of 50°, the water will travel farther than at any other angle.

Materials

▶ garden hose
▶ plastic table
▶ protractor
▶ measuring tape
   camera

Research Sources

▶ physics teacher
▶ firefighters
▶ science magazines or articles
▶ Related topics: water pressure, gravity, fluid dynamics, fluid flow

This experiment should be done outdoors.

Procedure

1. Turn on the hose and do not turn it off during the experiment. This will help ensure that the water pressure will be the same for all conditions. If you notice a drop or increase in pressure, be sure to note it in your journal.

2. Rest the hose on the edge of the table so that the water will fall onto the grass or concrete surface. If the table is on a flat surface, the hose will be at a 0° angle from the ground when it is flat on the table. While a helper holds the hose flat against the table, use a tape measure to see what distance the water travels. Photograph or sketch the hose and water, and record the distance traveled.

3. Use a protractor to adjust the angle of the hose 10° upward. While the helper holds the hose at this angle, measure the distance the water travels this time. Photo or sketch and record as above.

4. Continue changing the angle of the hose by 10°, until the hose is at 80°. Record the distance the water travels at every 10° change.

5. Repeat this experiment at least 2 more times. You may wish to check to see if the distance varies depending on the time of day and the water flow rate. You can estimate if the flow rate has changed by measuring the time it takes to fill a bucket of water.

Results

What distance does the water travel at each angle from 0° to 80°? What was the angle of the hose when the water traveled the farthest? Does the distance vary depending on the rate of water flow or the time of day?

Display Hints

Draw a picture of a garden hose and use string to show how far the water traveled when held at the different angles. Use diagrams showing the water flow when the hose was held at different angles. Use different colors for each angle.

GOING FURTHER

Elementary Level

How do different hose nozzles affect the distance the water travels from a hose placed at the various angles with the ground?

Junior High Level

If you were designing an in-ground sprinkler system, at which angle would you place the nozzle head in order to cover the most ground? How do changes in the water pressure affect the distance the water travels? Design a device to measure the differences in flow rate.

INDEX

abstract (of experiment), 22
allergies, 33
aromatherapy claims, 41–42
backboard, 24–25, 26
balloon scattering confetti, 34–35
batteries, 27
best friend, working with, 12
body parts, 27
books and magazines, 23
buildings to withstand earthquake, 64–65
chemical safety information, 33
chicken bones and calcium, 39–40
Choroplast, 25
collections, 14
conclusion, 18, 23, 31
contract, 7
control, 18
controlled variable, 17
creative thinking, 11
data, 17, 31
demonstrations, 14
displays, 24, 26, 27, 29
errors, 19, 23
experiment, 14, 17, 22
expert, finding, 12–13
faking results, 19
fingerprint experiment, 36–38
free stuff, 13
geotropism, 50
good manners, 29
hose angle and area covered, 93–95

hypothesis, 16, 18
Internet, 9, 12, 15, 23
interview, 16, 23
introduction, of report, 22
inventions, 14
journal, 15
judges, 30–31
kites, 86–88
letter asking for help, 13
library, 15, 16
live organisms, 10, 28
magnets and video and audiotapes, 91–92
manipulated variable, 18, 20
measurement, 18
Mimosa pudica, 46–48
models, 14, 15
nails and pressure, 83–85
observation, 17
oil layer and evaporation of water, 73–74
oral presentation, 27, 29, 31
originality, 30
osmosis in egg, 43–45
paper: dissolving, 75–76; recycling, 77–79
parents, 8
phototropism, 50
pine cones and air humidity, 56–57
plants' sense of touch, 46–48
prejudging event, 7
price and value of household items, 80–82
problem, 16
projects, 14, 30

references, 23
repeatability, 18
report, writing, 22–23
research, 15
responding variable, 18, 20
results, 18, 19
safety do's and don'ts, 32–33
science celebrations, 7
scientific method, 15–18
seed shape and distance traveled, 53–55
seismograph experiment, 66–70
serendipity, 19
soap bubbles, 62–63
spares, 26
spelling, 23
star charts, 71–72
starch production in leaves, 51–52
studies and surveys, 14
table (for display), 26
tables, graphs, charts, 20–21
teachers, 5–7
television programs, 16
timetable, 8
title, 22
toilet paper, 75–76
topics, 10, 11–12
tropisms in plants, 49–50
type, for signs, 27
variables, 17–18, 30
videotape, 30
volunteers, 27
water's freezing 58–59, 60–61
weight in and out of water, 89–90